HARNESSED FOR ADVENTURE

FOREWORD BY MIKE PILAVACHI

HARNESSED

True Life Stories Of

FOR

Faith Adventures With God

ADVENTURE

BY

GORDON HICKSON

Produced By

HEARTCRY
FOR CHANGE

www.heartcryforchange.com

A Publication by Heartcry Ministries
Heartcry Ministries I CMS House I Watlington Road I Oxford I OX4 6BZ I UK

Heartcry Trust UK Registered Charity 1076993 (www.heartcryforchange.com)

ISBN: 978-0-9837641-6-8

HARNESSED FOR ADVENTURE
True Life Stories Of Faith Adventures With God
by Gordon Hickson

Book cover and content layout designed by David Hickson

Edited by the Heartcry Publishing Team

Proof Read by Pauline Azer

First Edition – Printed September 2019

What Others Say

"Gordon and Rachel Hickson are both well known to me. We stood, arm in arm, and shoulder to shoulder, working for several years in God's ripest harvest fields. Gordon was for a time the Crusade Director of *Christ for all Nations* – a true man of faith, with width and depth. Their stories match the Acts of the Apostles. *Harnessed for Adventure* is a fitting title for this great book. It is breath-taking, amazing and glorifying God. I highly recommend it. Everyone should have it."

Evangelist Reinhard Bonnke, Christ for All Nations

—

"Gordon and Rachel Hickson are two of the most genuine followers of Jesus I've ever met. Their heart for God and their heart for people is legendary. I admire them both so deeply that I find it easy to recommend Harnessed for Adventure. This book is an engaging memoir of their journey with God, which is filled with ups and downs, twists and turns, and constant supernatural interventions that only a wonderful Heavenly Father could do. While this book reveals their inspiring walk with God, it even more reveals our God as a perfect Father. Read, enjoy, be inspired, and watch out...this lifestyle is contagious!"

Bill Johnson, Senior Pastor Bethel Church, Redding, CA, USA

—

"Harnessed for Adventure is profoundly eye-opening. Gordon Hickson's story will deeply touch its readers on many levels. For those searching for God, it will answer their questions. Also, the beautiful threads of how God weaves even difficult circumstances for our good is impactful. The story of God's miraculous healing when our bodies are broken and we are in despair will impart faith to all who go on the adventure to delve into these pages."

Dr. Cindy Jacobs, Generals International

"Legacy is no small thing ... and when you encounter a family wherein legacy is part of their history and landscape, you desire to know more. Gordon (and his wife, Rachel) have a story to tell... and the fruit that I am most familiar with, is that of their daughter, Nicola, who, many years ago, came to our leadership college in Sydney and then married one of the young men in our world. Together, they now lead our Melbourne (and Victorian) Hillsong rooms.

I share of Gordon's daughter because children often bear greatest witness to one's life. I recently listened to Nicola speak of her parents – their faith and their exploits, and in particular the unseen passion and devotion of her father. Listening made me want to read and know more of this pioneering couple. I am confident that this book, "Harnessed for Adventure", will intrigue and inspire you also and give you courage to follow the God dreams within."

BOBBIE HOUSTON, CO-GLOBAL SENIOR PASTOR, HILLSONG CHURCH

—

"This excellent book begins with high drama that seems to expand with each chapter. I was amazed at how many powerful and faith-filled stories are contained within its pages. Stories covering nations, relationships, conversions, healings, missions, spiritual warfare and substantiated miracles. All of these point towards the adventure journey of two people determined to live life to the full in total abandonment to the will of God."

STUART BELL, SENIOR LEADER, GROUNDLEVEL NETWORK

—

"Gordon and Rachel are such precious friends who we've journeyed with for decades now and we know that they are the real deal. They've experienced the massive highs and lows of frontline ministry and have come through with so much to teach us, whilst still retaining a beautiful passion for Jesus and His church."

ANDY & MICHELE HAWTHORNE, FOUNDER/DIRECTORS OF THE MESSAGE TRUST

"Obedience to God is not just a high calling, it always leads to unexpected adventures. The adventures Rachel and Gordon have lived through are an inspiration, and an illustration that there is nothing better than surrendering our future to the Lordship of Christ. I have the highest regard for Gordon and Rachel and, through this book, we can all get to know them better."

LYNN GREEN, YWAM GLOBAL PRESIDENT

—

"Harnessed for Adventure tells the amazing faith-filled story of two wonderful followers of Jesus - Gordon and Rachel Hickson. The book is their story, but it will inspire many to embark on the adventure of surrender to whatever God might ask of us next."

STEVE CLIFFORD, GENERAL DIRECTOR OF THE EVANGELICAL ALLIANCE

—

"I pray that these stories will germinate infectious seeds of hope and faith in your lives, and that this book will serve to mobilize a new movement of radical and passionate youth 'harnessed for adventures' with Jesus!"

PETE GREIG, FOUNDER, 24/7 PRAYER MOVEMENT

—

"I have supported Gordon for several years as a Patron of Mahabba: I know personally the faith needed in the countries and situations in which he and Rachel have been involved, so I highly recommend this challenging and inspiring book. May it spur on many to step out into adventures with God!"

THE BARONESS COX, FOUNDER /CEO, HUMANITARIAN AID RELIEF TRUST

—

"Gordon and Rachel have been long-standing friends and are great Kingdom pioneers. I so appreciate their passion for the Lord, and their faithfulness to His purposes."

DAVE SMITH, SENIOR PASTOR, KINGSGATE COMMUNITY CHURCH

"Gordon and Rachel are an extraordinary couple, who have done extraordinary things, sold-out-serving their extraordinary Jesus."

SIMON PONSONBY, ST ALDATES CHURCH, OXFORD

AND THE FINAL WORD GOES TO OUR KIDS...!

"Gordon Hickson is known and fiercely loved by many around the world. He has mentored, pastored, discipled, trained and most importantly loved and believed in people, helping them to step into their God adventures and callings.

However, to me, Gordon Hickson is first and foremost my Dad, my hero, the one who made it easy for me to understand an unconditional love of a heavenly father because he emulates this with his entire life.

A legacy of faith, perseverance, tenacity and passion for the cause of Christ marks Gordon's life. A man of impeccable integrity and a robust resilience who has an unswerving passion for God and his people.

This book tells a magnificent story of a life lived in total surrender to God, an Ephesians 3v20 kind of life. As you read this book you will be inspired to dream bigger, believe God is able to do anything and that you can also be a part of God's master story he is penning on planet earth. The life my Dad, Gordon Hickson, has lived is an example to all of what walking with Jesus can and should be like.

Your adventure awaits!"

NICOLA DOUGLASS, PASTOR HILLSONG MELBOURNE CITY CAMPUS

—

"I could justifiably use a plethora of superlatives to try to describe Dad's character but, in short, he is my hero. Thanks to his and my mother's relentless, selfless and courageous pursuit of faith, my life has been eternally impacted to expect the supernatural in my everyday in the knowledge that our limitless God can, and wants to, do immeasurably more than we can ask or imagine.

Now a father myself, I have the privilege of teaching the next generation to see the impossible as just another opportunity for God to be glorified through our story, something I can only do thanks to my parents' example.

Their names may not be as widely known as some of those who've given commendations in this book but there will be countless generations around the globe who will know the name of Jesus because of their utterly committed pursuit of sharing the Gospel, equipping leaders, birthing and supporting ministries and standing in faith and in partnership with Heaven to see the miraculous love of Jesus transform individuals, homes, churches, communities, regions and nations.

Theirs is a legacy of such worth and magnitude, one simply cannot quantify it – and what's exciting is that our generation has the privilege of using this as a foundation from which to launch out on our own adventures of faith. So let's be expectant for God to do more, immeasurably more!"

DAVID HICKSON, FINANCIAL ANALYST

Preface & Dedication

This is my first book and it seeks to capture something of the incredible thrill of living a life totally abandoned to Jesus. It is obviously our life story and told through my own personal filters of perception and memory of events. I have tried, as faithfully as possible, to record both the highs and the lows, the excitements and challenges, on the roller-coaster of our lives. Unfortunately, as you get older, memory can become selective! So, if in any part of the book I have failed to recall all the details correctly, please forgive me, and graciously look beyond the exact details and allow yourself to be overwhelmed instead by the greater story of the extraordinary love and faithfulness of our Father God that I seek to portray.

I dedicate this book to my precious wife, Rachel, who has inspired me with her writing over the last twelve years. She has lived, loved, and learned through all that God has taken us through, and has become one of the most gifted communicators of the heart and dreams of God for individuals, communities, and nations.

I also want to express my sincere gratitude to her parents who, to a large extent, helped fashion and shape me spiritually. God has been so good to us and, as you read through these amazing stories of the adventures which God has led us on, we pray that you will also be gripped with a radical desire to make your life count through a relentless surrender to God's plan and call.

This is obviously our story together and so we both dedicate our life story to the next generation of our wonderful kids and grandkids who are already experiencing their own adventures with God. There is no greater sense of fulfilment and joy than knowing that our next two generations have grabbed hold of the baton and are already running with us, shoulder to shoulder, in this thrilling race of life with the Holy Spirit.

CONTENTS

What Others Say 7

Preface & Dedication 13

Foreword 19

Chapter 01 - **A DONKEY FOR JESUS** 21

Chapter 02 - **ABORTED ATTEMPTS** 29

Chapter 03 - **HIJACKED IN THE ITALIAN ALPS** 35

Chapter 04 - **CAMBRIDGE REVIVAL AND ESKIMO ENCOUNTER** 41

Chapter 05 - **GERMAN ENCOUNTERS** 47

Chapter 06 - **IRISH SHOWDOWN** 53

Chapter 07 - **SURPRISED BY LOVE!** 59

Chapter 08 - **KOREAN FAITH** 67

Chapter 09 - **THE AFRICA CALL** 75

Chapter 10 - **THE MALAWI MIRACLE** 83

Chapter 11 - **KENYA AND WORLD HORIZONS** 89

Chapter 12 - **WHEN GOD SHOWS HIS FINGERPRINTS** 99

Chapter 13 - **RELUCTANT HOMECOMING** 107

Chapter 14 - **CHURCH AND KINGDOM – CITIES FOR CHRIST** 115

Chapter 15 - **FIRE FROM HEAVEN** 121

Chapter 16 - **RELEASING GOD'S HEARTCRY** 129

Chapter 17 - **DRAWN TO THE ARCTIC** 135

Chapter 18 - **THE MUSLIM WORLD AND BACK TO JERUSALEM** 145

Chapter 19 - **LONDON CALLING** 151

Chapter 20 - **GOD'S PASSION FOR RECONCILIATION** 159

Chapter 21 - **THE GLOBAL PRAYER AND PROPHETIC MOVEMENT** 167

Chapter 22 - TIME TO CROSS THE POND 175

Chapter 23 - CALLED AS A SHEPHERD TO OXFORD 183

Chapter 24 - FOR MILLIONS OF MUSLIMS TO KNOW HIM 191

Chapter 25 - CALLED TO THE MARGINS TO REACH THE BROKEN.........199

Chapter 26 - UNBLOCKING THE WELL OF MIRACLES AND REVIVAL 209

Chapter 27 - FINISHING THE RACE – WELL ADJUSTED.....................217

Books by Rachel Hickson 225

FOREWORD

I will never forget the first time I met Gordon Hickson. It was one of the significant encounters of my life. Twenty-seven years ago, the Lord spoke to eleven of us to move to Watford to plant a church in order to reach unchurched young people. One of the things I needed to do was visit many of the local clergy to explain our vision, assure them that we had no desire to steal their young people but indeed to serve the town alongside them. It was not going well. Many were angry, felt threatened and could not understand what we were trying to do. One significant church leader was particularly hostile and indeed rude to us and about us.

Then I met Gordon. He led probably the largest church in Watford and certainly the liveliest! I was expecting another difficult and discouraging conversation. Instead, all I received was kindness and grace. He listened to our story, asked some questions, and then, without hesitation, welcomed us into the town and assured us of his and Rachel's full support. One of the comments he made staggered me and is something that has remained with me over the years. He said, "I will tell my church about you and we will pray for you and support you in any way we can. I will tell our young people to come and support you in all you are doing. We will probably lose our young people to you as a result, but I don't care. As long as the kingdom of God is being built!"

I was staggered. And Gordon meant every word. For the next few years he was our champion, our support, and our cheerleader. He provided us with a place to meet, prayed for us, gave us incredibly wise advice and spoke positively to the other church leaders on our behalf.

Years later I asked Gordon why he had decided to spend so much time and energy supporting us. He responded that when they had arrived in Watford they faced a good deal of hostility and opposition from some other churches. He did some historical research and discovered that Watford had quite a history of disunity between churches. As they prayed, he and Rachel discerned a principality of division over the town. So they committed to do some spiritual warfare until the demonic stronghold was broken. And they didn't only pray. They lived in the opposite spirit. They befriended their enemies and loved them until they gave up and became friends! We are the beneficiaries of this.

I write this to say Gordon is the real deal. That which he writes about, he lives with passion, integrity and humility. I loved reading this book. Gordon does not gloss over the struggles and painful times and, indeed, the seeming failures. Yet, in reading these pages, I believe you will come away inspired, encouraged and filled with faith to pursue our dependable yet unpredictable God. You will also be taught and informed about the kindness, grace and commitment of our Saviour both for us and his world.

A great book for all those who want to move from existing in security to living in adventure.

MIKE PILAVACHI, FOUNDER/DIRECTOR OF SOUL SURVIVOR

1

A Donkey For Jesus

My wife, Rachel, had the last laugh as she had always said that my problem was stubbornness but I had just called it "being persistent"! But there I was, attending a Businessmen's Lunch during the Christ for all Nations's (CfaN's) crusade in Harare, Zimbabwe in October 1984. The preacher, a German evangelist called Reinhard Bonnke, took up his Bible and began to read from Matthew chapter 21, about Jesus sending his disciples to untie the donkey so that he could ride into Jerusalem; using this scripture, he began to encourage the business people present to release their "tethered assets" for God's mission.

Suddenly he shouted out, "Loose this ass, the Lord has need of him!". As these words resounded across the room, it was as if he was shouting directly at me - as if God was grabbing hold of my stubborn donkey ears and shaking me. I don't remember another thing he said as all I could hear was God shouting into my spirit, "If only you will surrender your stubbornness and obey my call, you too - like that donkey - will carry My glory from city to city."

This was the defining moment in which I can truly say that I not only heard the call of God but I finally and wholeheartedly surrendered to

God's plan for my life. I returned later that evening to our Youth With A Mission (YWAM) accommodation in Cork Road, Harare, and my wife immediately asked, "What on earth has just happened to you? You look white!" I quickly blurted out the events of the evening, explaining that God had just got hold of me and that we were going to sell up everything in the UK and move to Zimbabwe to join the Christ for all Nations team.

It was a remarkable moment of spiritual significance. However, within 24 hours, I was lying unconscious in a Zimbabwean hospital with my pelvis smashed, and seemingly paralyzed with a spinal injury. My wife, Rachel, was even worse and, once I regained consciousness, I was told by the doctors that both her legs were severely fractured and that she was now in a terminal coma due to multiple fat embolisms resulting from the fatty material from her broken legs that had moved through her heart and lungs and was now lodged in her brain stem. There was minimal brain activity so they gave her a 5% chance of survival, but then probably only as a "vegetable" due to the oxygen starvation of the brain.

All this was the result of having rushed to the scene of a car crash outside our accommodation just after we returned from the Bonnke crusade meeting the night after the Businessmen's Lunch. President Mugabe's personal aide and three cabinet ministers had crashed into their own police escort. Miraculously, on Rachel's insistence, I had unstrapped our 6-month-old baby, Nicola, from the baby pouch on my front and placed her into her cot before we rushed out to help. The personal aide was dying in the driver's seat from the impact injuries where the steering wheel had rammed into his chest, breaking his ribs, so I rushed back into the house to grab a crowbar to enable us to open the driver's car door. While all this was in process, another driver stopped to help at the accident. We discovered this man just happened to be an Accident and Emergency doctor from Warwick hospital, visiting his family in Zimbabwe, and he immediately took charge, taking the crowbar from me to open the door of the car.

Suddenly we began to hear shouts of alarm and, as we turned to look behind us, we just caught sight of a 7-ton military vehicle hurtling towards us, before it then smashed into all three of us. I was hit in the back and pelvis and was thrown unconscious onto the verge of the road; the medical doctor was literally skewered by the crowbar which went right through him, and Rachel was then sandwiched between this truck and the car. As she was being dragged down the road, both her legs were shattered underneath her. She was conscious throughout this whole process and calling out in prayer for Jesus to help us.

Unbeknown to Rachel, a Christian family who lived on that road junction, also cried out to God for help as soon as they heard the first crash. However, in the midst of the chaos on the road, we were still totally unaware of the miracles that were about to take place in answer to all those prayers. Several of the CfaN team members also heard about the crash and rushed to the scene. I was picked up from the verge, unconscious and paralyzed, and carefully transported with the injured doctor by ambulance to the nearby hospital; Rachel was transported later in a private car and arrived at the same hospital. Disaster had struck but God was beginning to work to turn this attack into a springboard into ministry.

That night, as I lay there unconscious, God miraculously touched my spine, but strangely not my pelvis. The next morning the doctors came onto my ward looking confused and asked me if I had ever broken my spine previously, as I seemed to have scar tissue of about 8 years in age indicating an earlier break in my spine. I explained that I had never broken my spine and that eight or so years ago I had been on a cross-country ski team in the army! The hospital had also examined the British doctor and found that the crowbar had "bent" its way round all the major organs in his body - he was released a week later with a band-aid on his front and a bandage on his back!

My wife, Rachel, had the broken bones in both her legs carefully realigned and was then plastered from the tips of her toes to the top of her thighs. Miraculously, her upper body was remarkably undamaged, except for a couple of cracked ribs, despite receiving the full impact from the 7-ton truck. As Rachel often says, "There must have been a few dented Angels that night!" However, within a few hours, she suddenly felt intense pain in her heart, lungs and head, and then sank into a deep coma due to the fat emboli moving through her bloodstream.

The day before, the doctors had treated a similar case and had had to leave this patient to die on a side ward as there was no hope of recovery; so Rachel, with minimal brain activity, was similarly wheeled into this side ward to await death. I have to say that it was a strange four days of waiting and watching beside her bed. It sounds rather silly but I had absolute faith and confidence that she would not die: and it was very real. I held on to the fact that we had made a simple child-like promise to each other when we married that we would never die and go to be with Jesus without the other one.

On the fifth day, Rachel's parents flew out to Zimbabwe, knowing that they might be coming to collect her body and taking charge of their granddaughter, Nicola, too. She was now being looked after by the team of YWAM girls who were doing their best to feed this 5-month-old baby. Rachel's parents were in turmoil as they stood in the hospital room but, as people of faith, something bold rose up inside them and her Dad suddenly shouted out from Psalm 118, "You shall not die but live, and you will proclaim what the Lord has done!", as he looked at his lifeless daughter.

Within 5 hours of this prayer, to the utter shock of the doctors and nurses, Rachel regained consciousness and came out of this deep terminal coma! She recalls that moment vividly: she was suddenly wide awake and looking out of the window in amazement at the intense purple colour of the jacaranda trees. As she looked around in wonder at everything in the room, she suddenly saw the Zimbabwean nurse leap to her feel in shock and charge out of the room, hitting the large swing doors with force on her way out. The sight of her very ample backside bursting through those doors made Rachel laugh!

Very soon a cohort of doctors and nurses rushed into the room: they tested and re-tested her brain function with various challenges such as making her read childish books like, "This is Peter and this is Jane". They then tested her memory and examined every other indicator. There was only one conclusion: this was a total miracle as there was no brain damage of any kind. Eventually the doctors gave her a certificate that she was "brain normal". Sadly I don't have one, so Rachel has the upper hand whenever the family challenges her! I was carried through this entire episode with that simple gift of faith which God gave me as she slipped away into the coma. But now my darling Rachel was back again, and we were soon overwhelmed with countless people who came to see the miracle for themselves.

There was one thing which had intrigued the doctors during those days in the coma. A recently converted Zimbabwean girl from our church wanted to see Rachel healed so she read all the healing Scriptures she could find from the Bible onto a cassette tape. Feeling that she was unable to pray effectively, she decided to stay with Rachel night and day, faithfully restarting and turning the cassette over and over to feed the Word of God into Rachel's spirit. The doctors were fascinated and asked, "What is this power? Whenever we turn this cassette off, your wife just 'flat lines' with no brain activity but, as soon as we replace the earphones, her brain activity responds again!" They could watch her brain respond to the sound of the Word of God on this tape! Surely in every way God was showing his miraculous healing power and we both were living miracles.

We heard many years later from one of the Zimbabwean prayer leaders that hundreds of Christians had also been praying night and day for a miracle for us. At that time, we had joined a wonderful praying church called Hear the Word Church which was led by Tom and Bonnie Deuschle. This church was not only a praying church but also a faith-filled church. They, together with thousands of others, believed God would do miracles that night.

The miracles continued as streams of Government officials came to see us and thank us for rescuing the three cabinet ministers from the first accident, though sadly Mugabe's personal aide, Jinx Ndongwe, had died of his injuries. The CfaN team had become very well known in the city, as thousands of people had surrendered their lives to Jesus in our meetings, including Sally Mugabe, the President's wife, and her niece.

So we were thrilled when Sally Mugabe visited us and offered to help us in any way possible. Then, two weeks into our recovery, President Mugabe personally arranged for 18 seats to be booked on a BA flight home to London. This enabled us to be transported on stretchers on this flight, safely hidden behind curtains, resting over these many seats. We were also honoured that an off-duty BA stewardess took special leave and offered to take care of our little baby, Nicola, and travelled with us the whole way back to London.

The final miracle that happened was unusual favour for the CfaN team. Just before the accident, the permits of two ministries we worked closely with had been withdrawn, severely restricting our ability to work in the country. However, during one of these hospital visits, the Government ministers promised to remove all restrictions from these ministries as well as allowing Christ for all Nations (CfaN) to organize our first Fire Conference in 1986, when 4000 evangelists came to Harare from across Africa to catch the evangelistic fire of God. YWAM were similarly given governmental help with all their activities.

This stubborn donkey had finally surrendered, and God was now able to harness me into His perfect will. Every attempt of the devil to thwart the plans of God for our lives had not only failed but had, in fact, released a far greater impetus to commit totally to His call. But this journey of teaching me to yield to God's ways had taken time because I was brought up in a privileged, self-centred bubble.

2

ABORTED ATTEMPTS

To say that I was rather arrogant and independent - in fact a "piece of work" - was an understatement. I grew up Anglo-Irish, as part of the Protestant ascendency class who dominated Ireland from the 17th to 20th century as landowners, professionals, Protestant clergy and lawyers. In fact, my great-great-grandfather had been Lord Chancellor of Ireland. I remember my Dad half-joking that he had expected to live in a castle when he grew up, as his mother had remarried into the Barrington family after his father's early death. They owned Glenstal Castle in Limerick which eventually became a very exclusive private school.

My paternal grandfather, who had died early, had been an Officer in the Indian army and was in one of the last mounted Cavalry charges in the North West Frontier of India. My father was also a highly decorated British Army Officer who was awarded the MBE and Military Cross for extreme gallantry during the Second World War. His family were very much British Empire background and he was born in Lahore (now Pakistan). My mother's family were Crawfords, from a similar background, and she was born in Bombay, India, where her father served as Director of Bombay Electric Company.

The hidden aspects of my past were only revealed many years later: my Scottish grandfather, who had been born in 1864, had sadly separated from his first wife and five children when they returned to Switzerland - she had never wanted to return to India due to the intolerable conditions of living in Bombay at that time. He continued living in the paddy fields of Andheri, Bombay: it was a lonely and empty life, which he filled with inventions, writing poetry, and playing the cello, until he fell in love many years later with a young German/Danish girl who used to come and take care of his housework. My mother was the only child of this second marriage. Clara Benzien-Moeller, my maternal grandmother, was in fact from Schleswig Holstein and was born in Hamburg so now this German/Danish blood was flowing in my veins!

What was remarkable though is that, during those lonely years, my grandfather found God and became an ardent student of the Bible. My mother recalled that she too gave her life to Jesus at the age of 7 as she sat on her dad's lap. The scene was being set for God's eternal plans: forty years later, a young British missionary couple were called by God to move across to Bombay and based themselves about a mile away from the home of my grandfather in Andheri (now a concrete jungle). Unsuspecting, their young daughter, Rachel, grew up there, unaware that she would one day marry the grandson of this pioneer engineer who had lived just down the road, but in another generation.

Though God had His eternal plans, it seemed that the devil was equally determined to thwart those plans. My mother married my father while he was Brigade Major in Rangoon, Burma, overseeing the repatriation of the Japanese prisoners of war. After their tour of duty in Burma they returned to UK with their two children. However, before she became pregnant for a third time, she was cursed by a gypsy who told my mother that she would never have a third child and if she tried, she would die. My mum did almost die in childbirth, but she survived and gave birth to me, her third and final child.

Though the blessing of God was visibly on me from the start, clouds were gathering to abort God's plans for my life. Though born in Carlisle, I grew up for several years on a British base in Germany, before my father was posted to Aden, now South Yemen, to oversee the movement of British troops during the first Kuwait Crisis. This left several indelible memories: firstly, that I only saw my parents for a few weeks each school year during the summer holidays when I would be flown across the world to see them – this was emotionally damaging and daunting at the tender age of seven. The rest of the year I was either at boarding school, or stayed with my uncle and aunt on their farm near Carbury in the south of Ireland, where we created incredibly happy memories, in spite of the separation from my parents.

The second memory was that my mother was initially unable to join my father in Aden, South Yemen, so she took a job as the matron in a girls' school. So my first experience of school was as the only boy at a small girls' boarding school in Netheravon! Maybe this explains my later reticence to get married, or perhaps it helped me to really understand how girls tick! After the initial shock of this new environment it actually became an idyllic time. Every morning I was able to get up early and ride the school horses across Salisbury Plain. My love of horses stemmed from this time.

I later transitioned to a wonderful preparatory school (Junior School), and then Wellington College in Crowthorne, Berkshire, where I excelled as "Victor Ludorum" (Top Athlete) at many sports and was always top of the class. Sadly, being educated in a private school which was set up to groom boys for leadership in the British Empire, created an arrogant independence in me which would take years to harness. By the time I left school at the end of the 1960s, the British Empire was no more, and a whole generation of boys was impacted with the rebellion, drink and drugs culture that was to grip Britain in the 60s. The plans and purposes of God in my life could well have been aborted just as many of my friends' lives were ruined during this time.

However, having failed to infect me with this abortive rebellion and drug culture, the enemy took a different route: I was very intelligent, and passionately focused on finding the reasons for life. I was therefore intrigued one day to hear a radio programme called "The World Tomorrow" broadcast by an American cult called the Worldwide Church of God (WWCG). I was gripped with an addictive passion and obsession to listen to their programmes and began to get up early at 4am every morning to study the Bible - it was however through their cultic lens and it would take years to recalibrate my mind.

The fanaticism of this cult required you to obey numerous rules and regulations rather than having a relationship with Jesus. We were trained to pay lip service to Jesus but then it became obligatory to keep many rules and observances, particularly various Jewish food laws and a strict Sabbath. My naïve obsessions came to a crisis point at Wellington College when I refused to participate in any activities on Saturdays, as well as abstaining from certain foods.

I am so thankful for two people who rescued me: firstly, the headmaster, Frank Fisher, son of a former Archbishop of Canterbury, who simply called me to his office and said he respected my choice, but it was incompatible with the school – I would have to leave! This bombshell brought me back to reality and I apologized to him and began to live a divided life - believing one thing but having to live another.

The other rescuer was my House Master, Peter (POG) White, who had a Theology Doctorate and offered to meet with me privately for a term. He proposed that we should discuss all the teachings of the cult and, if my obsession was not proven to be wrong, he would then be prepared to join the cult. I was so arrogant that I thought I would convert him. In actual fact, by the end of the term, I was so confused and disillusioned that I slammed the door on this cult and instead threw myself into just finishing school well. I then excelled, ending up as a Prefect, Deputy Head of School, Captain of Rugby and on many other teams. However, I was one of the only pupils to join the army from this military feeder school as others were influenced by the cultural shift of 1960s anti-establishment.

One of the sad fruits from these three years of cultic obsession was that I converted my older brother to the cult before I "saw the light". I lived with this sense of guilt for many years, having incurred the wrath of my distinguished military father who said he would never forgive me for ruining my brother's life. Due to my persuasive character, my brother had left the British Army and enrolled himself at the WWCG Bible School in Bricket Wood. He spent almost 20 years with them before he was miraculously rescued, along with thousands of the WWCG: they have since become the first cult to repent at the top levels and retrain all their ministers in an Evangelical Bible School. Along with many others, my brother had a revelation of Jesus and the Cross and within two years was serving God in the Ukraine.

Somehow, what the devil intended for harm was eventually turned by God into a wonderful plan for my brother's life. Years later, I was even able to receive my father's forgiveness and witness my Dad receiving Jesus into his life. That was a moment I had been longing for and it brought a deep sense of family restoration.

However, due to this chaotic episode in my life, I had become unsure about my future. Despite being offered excellent places at several great universities, I made a calculated decision to escape into the army, and activated an Army Scholarship to Sandhurst which I had won at the age of 13. Little did I know that these army years were to become part of the formative plan of God to reshape my life and character, as he prepared to harness me for His plan for my life. We tend to think of harnessing in terms of a rider harnessing a horse but, as a climber, I needed to take the responsibility of adjusting my own harness to secure me to the Anchor Point. I needed to secure myself to God's anchor, before He could then harness me for His plan and call.

3

Hijacked In The Italian Alps

Before I take you to the Italian Alps, let me first set the scene and context of my world at that time: I had just arrived at the Royal Military Academy Sandhurst, as part of Intake 48. This was the last 2-year Officer Training course conducted at Sandhurst. I was 19 years old, super fit, arrogant, independent and full of myself.

I will never forget the huge frame of the Academy Sergeant Major hovering over me as he glowered at all the new intake: "Let's get one thing straight!", he bellowed in my face, "I call you 'Sir', and you call me 'Sir', but remember this: ONLY ONE OF US MEANS THIS, SIR!" I don't know about the "fear of God", but my goodness, every one of us shook with the fear of attracting the wrath of this man who was to shape our lives over the next two years.

Sandhurst Military Academy is probably one of the most effective Military Training Academies in the world. Governments globally were sending their most promising young officers to train alongside us. The whole training system is designed to totally deconstruct every individual during the first term, waking us up at unearthly times of the night and forcing us to do mindless tasks. As with most pressure situations, it was often our British sense of humour which kept us sane. I recall during one of these middle of the night wake up calls, the sergeant shouted for us all to stand to attention at our doors, wearing only one item of clothing: one brave friend emerged standing to attention with just a bow tie strategically tied round his privates. The rest of us now struggled to maintain our salute as we internally collapsed in laughter. The aim in all these mindless exercises was to bring every individual to respond with instant obedience to the slightest command!

During the remaining months of the first year and second year, they rebuilt and shaped each person into a seamless unit of military excellence. Whether we liked it or not, each person became stamped in the image and nature of a British Army Officer. I was in my element and loving every moment. It certainly toughened each of us, though sadly one of our cadets was killed during the training.

At the end of the first year, my passion for adventure resurfaced: I applied for extended leave to drive all the way from London to Northern Iran (about 4000 miles just to get there!). Ever since my time in Wellington College, I had been intrigued by the idea of exploring the Castles of the Assassins up in the Alamut Valley, hidden in the Elburz mountains.

The Military Academy kindly lent me a new long-wheel based Land Rover, and I persuaded three close friends to join me in the adventure. It took us about a week to drive to Tehran, and then we headed off up north into the mountains on dirt tracks and riverbeds. To be honest, I have no idea how we survived: several times we were totally bogged down, and each time we were rescued by locals with their strong bullocks.

It was an extraordinary time as these valleys look as if they are in a time warp, thousands of years behind modern times! The castles themselves were obviously in ruins, but as we scaled the mountains to look at the ruins, we realized how terrifying it must have been for the whole of Persia to be intimidated by these killers (hence the name Assassin), drugged by Hashish. These castles were so hidden and impregnable that it took years before a fighting force was able to conquer these drug-fuelled war-lords.

In my second year at Sandhurst, due to my gift for languages, I was asked to learn Russian in one year, to prepare me for the Cold War environment of the 70s which I was about to step into. Almost fifty years later, I can hardly remember any Russian, although after that year of study, I was comfortable conversing in Russian and even reading Yevtushenko poetry in Russian!

It was such an honour, at the end of these two years, to graduate in front of my father who retired that year from the army as a Colonel: during the Passing Out Parade I was shocked to be presented with the Queen's Medal for the Cadet with the highest score in military, practical and academic studies. I was unaware at that time of someone else smiling that day: God, who would one day become my "Father God", was smiling too, knowing that I was being knocked into shape and moulded for His plan.

At Sandhurst, now free from the "hell hound" of religious confusion which had hounded me for the last few years, I had thrown myself into military life and activities. Three of the passions which I developed over this time were skiing, climbing and flying small private planes. I was soon spending all my free time in all these activities and it was not long before I had my Private Pilot's License and was accomplished in both climbing and skiing.

I was beginning to climb at "Extreme" level with my climbing partner who introduced me to the wonders of sheer rock buttresses in Snowdonia and Derbyshire. We took crazy risks but arrogantly thought we were invincible. I was beginning to live dangerously close to the edge so I am grateful for a small group of military intercessors, who cried out to God to save me for His purpose. I owe my life to those hidden, nameless intercessors, who committed themselves to pray for the armed forces and had received my name from the army chaplain.

The planning room of Heaven got to work, and I was soon on my way to a little village in Northern Italy called Livigno, where a Sandhurst ski team was being trained. I was unaware that I was about to be hijacked by Heaven! One of the team's trainers and leaders was a young staff major at Sandhurst called Zac Freeth, who had previously represented the UK as a skier in the Winter Olympics. He and his wife, Claire, had become committed Bible-believing Christians, and they decided to invite a young Christian evangelism team to Livigno to reach out to the Sandhurst team. I was really offended by these "God Squad" people and would regularly encourage my skiing team friends to disrupt their outreaches.

Christmas Day arrived and I naïvely accepted an invitation to celebrate Christmas in a little Italian chapel which they had hired for the evening. I will never forget how we sang a few carols and then Major Zac Freeth stood up and opened his Bible: he proceeded to preach, seemingly directly at me, for about 15 minutes. "What good is it", he quoted from the Bible, "if you gain the whole world and yet lose your own soul." I was infuriated! How dare anyone be so insensitive as to preach at people on Christmas Day of all days! An irritating grain of sand had somehow been sown into my "oyster": one day it would produce a priceless pearl, but right now it was creating within me an intense hatred of God and of any religion. This was probably fueled by the sense of failure and confusion which I was left with when I had slammed the door of my heart to God when I had left the WWCG cult in disillusionment to join the army. But, without knowing it, I had just been hijacked!

My first military posting was to 2nd Field Regiment, Royal Artillery, in Hemer, Germany. Much as I loved military life, I was still passionate about climbing and skiing, forming a close relationship with a young soldier who loved climbing: he had joined up as a "squaddie" to escape his narrow world of having become a world expert with a doctorate in some obscure aspect of fruit diseases. On our days off we attempted all kinds of difficult climbs, but I was soon called to account by the Commanding Officer who objected to a Commissioned Officer befriending a mere soldier!

It was the previous grain of outrage against the God Squad in Livigno, mixed with the outrage I now felt at the Colonel's attitude to this "squaddie" (who was on a highly superior level of intelligence than all of us Officers) which became a life-changing explosive mixture: an inner explosion was about to catapult me into the next arena of God's plan. I asked the Colonel respectfully if he would allow me to apply for an "In Service Scholarship" to university. I think he was delighted to see the back of me, so he willingly signed my application.

To my surprise, Cambridge University asked me to come for an interview but it's hard to believe my arrogance when, upon receiving their invitation, I simply replied that I was "too busy with military exercises and responsibilities" to be able to attend the interview. It has always puzzled me how on earth God engineered that the selection committee at Corpus Christi College still immediately offered me a place at the College. It was a decision that they would later regret, though they had no idea of the part they would play in my journey of being found by God.

I arrived in Cambridge in October 1973, a "mature" student of 22, driving a brand-new tax-free Audi which I had bought during my military tour in Hemer, Germany. All my college fees for the next three years were to be paid by the Army, including the payment of my basic salary. Life was great but reality hit me within a week when I realized that I would end up buying all the drinks! The car was very quickly sold and I was soon frequenting all the pubs and bars in tatty jeans and a scruffy jumper – and sometimes in bare feet! – and joining the masses cycling to and from lectures on an old rusty bike.

With the removal of all military discipline, my true nature began to surface, and over the first term I was drunk most evenings, and very soon in trouble with the police and my college Dean: I pursued my love of climbing by exploring the wonders of climbing the old stone colleges, churches, chapels and bridges, often in an inebriated state. I regularly climbed in and out of my college window.

The police finally caught up with me one night when I had rattled on the skylights of several students' rooms and boomed down, "Beware! The judgement of God is upon you!" It was also the era of "streaking", and I do remember vaguely through an intoxicated haze that I was caught by the college porters as I entered naked having streaked down the High Street after climbing up onto the roof of Kings College Chapel. "Mr. Hickson!", the Dean barked at me the next day, "we've come to a decision that you are too wild to live in College. For both our sanity, we would like you to move out of College into rented accommodation."

The scene was being set for a life-changing encounter with God as I then moved out of college to live on a houseboat, moored up at Jesus Lock. It was an idyllic location, and the perfect environment to start writing my personal dissertation to disprove Christianity and all religion. The fight was on!

4

CAMBRIDGE REVIVAL AND ESKIMO ENCOUNTER

The pace of my course enabled me to have ample time to dissect religion after religion, showing that every religion was just a mirror image of the social and cultural control system of that people group; this included religious Christianity, which I was soon enjoying pulling apart. I spent hours on this project due to the irritation of that little grain of sand implanted in me in the Italian Alps and I was thrilled when I completed it.

So imagine my horror when the "God-squad" students around me said, "Wonderful! You're so right about Religion. It stops so many millions from ever finding God. Real Christian faith isn't a religion, it's simply a precious relationship with Jesus Christ. God loved us so much that he sent His Son, Jesus, to die on our behalf, so that we wouldn't be excluded because of the mess we've made of our lives. The simple act of allowing Jesus to take control of our lives changes everything. God is suddenly right there as our Father – not a million miles away."

From that moment, Jesus himself became the focus of my fury. I read book after book to prove that he was a charlatan and a fraud.

However, I will be eternally grateful that one young Christian student, Henry Corbett, pursued me. It was just a few weeks into the spring term at Cambridge when I heard from Henry that a visiting evangelist called David MacInnes was due to spend a week in early February 1974 debating Jesus with the students. I used every means possible to dissuade students from attending these discussions but, like unsuspecting lemmings, they flocked to the Mission in their hundreds, and there seemed nothing I could do to stop them from falling over the edge into this religious abyss.

The day after the Mission finished, I sat down on my houseboat and continued to write more of my personal thoughts about why the Christian faith was an evil and deceptive cul-de-sac which had conned millions. I cannot truly explain what happened that evening but, as I continued to write furiously, suddenly the whole boat was filled with the presence of God!

I found myself on my knees, weeping, knowing that some powerful force was standing right there in front of me. My entire intellectual world was demolished in a moment and, after what seemed like an eternity, I got up from the floor and wrote on my paper: "I can never turn back. I know God is here, Jesus is alive and is the Son of God!" I threw on my coat and ran across town to Holy Trinity Church and sat at the back, still crying as I watched hundreds of students worshipping God.

Such was the intellectual bombshell that I grabbed my rucksack and just began walking for what seemed like days, trying to sort out my mind. However, after what was probably more like hours, I returned to my friends and joined the Christian Union and began to volunteer on the streets trying to help the homeless, alcoholics, and drug addicts. For the next few months I tried to live what I thought was an authentic Christian life but I rapidly became more and more depressed.

So, during my vacation, I escaped back to my love of climbing and travelled with my climbing mates to go "peak bagging". We travelled all the way up to Greenland to put our name on the unclimbed granite peaks, which towered above the icecap. It was right at the end of this expedition that I fell through the ice into a very deep crevasse. Miraculously, it seemed that the hand of God caught me and guided my fall onto a narrow snow bridge which held me until I could be found. Without this snow bridge, I would have fallen hundreds of feet, far beyond the reach of any rope, and to my death. I was aware once again that God had rescued me and had a purpose for my life.

Back in Cambridge for a second academic year, I threw myself into my studies but was still haunted by this low-lying depression. Now, if God can speak through a donkey, he certainly spoke to me through an Irish alcoholic I had befriended. One day towards the end of the summer term, this drunken rogue turned to me and said, "To be sure, you're a total hypocrite! At least I am filled with a lot of spirit, but you have absolutely nothing in you!" His words hit me like a ton of bricks. I knew it all in my head, and I had all my theology lined up, but still absolutely nothing had dropped into my heart and life – I felt nothing – I did not feel God's Spirit inside me.

It was a moment of reckoning, and I was relieved to be able to escape this moment of truth and rejoin my regiment in Canada for training exercises during my summer vacation. After the military exercises were completed, I still had two months' further vacation left before university started again. So I hitch-hiked on small planes all the way up the west coast of Canada to Whitehorse and then Inuvik, finally landing on the beach of the most northerly Eskimo village on the Arctic Ocean, a little place called Tuktoyaktuk – Tuk for short. What a joy to be a million miles away from all my confusion and spiritual depression! At last I had escaped from this whole God thing.

A small group of Eskimo boys gathered round me and took me to the village Head, but as we walked past the open door of one of their huts, I glanced in and saw a small group of Eskimos with their hands in the air singing and worshipping God! No way! How did God get here before me?

For a few weeks I managed to avoid these believers and worked for the village Head, helping build pre-fab houses; but then I was arrested by a Mountie Policeman and flown back to Inuvik, where I was kept under house arrest, accused of being a military deserter. Apparently they had heard talk of a British army officer living up in Tuk and had made a wrong assumption that I must be a deserter as I did look rather dishevelled. Even though I pleaded my innocence and tried to explain the situation, it was three days before they finally came to me, red-faced, and apologized that my story had checked out. However, it all turned out for the good as I was flown, free of charge, back to Medicine Hat in South Canada, where I then caught a further free military flight back home to the UK.

It was October 1975 and I was now back at university for my final year. I devoured the Bible day after day but I must admit that I attended no lectures for several weeks as I was gripped with this desperation to finally settle my God dilemma. It was as if God was willing to wait until all my pride and independence was exhausted, and I was desperate enough to honestly listen.

I will never forget the night when I was reading the Bible once again and this time God broke in. It was not an audible voice, but I "heard" His voice saying, "How can you really know me anyway, and be filled with me? It's not by believing in me, because the devil believes, and he trembles. You'll only know me intimately if you totally surrender your life into my hands – all the good and all the bad." I was so desperate, this was an offer I could not refuse any longer, and on that night in October 1975, as I wept, I totally surrendered my life to God and immediately I was flooded with the warm power of the Holy Spirit from head to toe. I felt Him fill me.

My life totally changed overnight and God led me to a little church on the outskirts of Cambridge called St Matthews, where Revd Sydney Simms, the Vicar, took me in hand. As adult baptisms were not allowed by the Anglicans in those days, he took me out to a little Baptist Church in Isleham where Spurgeon, the great preacher, was baptized, and there I was immersed in the baptism tank, together with a Catholic. As an Irish Protestant, who had been told that I would be disowned if I ever fraternized with Catholics, this moment sealed my passion for reconciliation in Christ. Years later I would find myself working shoulder to shoulder with Spirit-filled Catholics who are often the most passionate and radical believers.

My final two terms were a haze of glory: yes, I did finally graduate in Social Psychology and Social Anthropology, but my greatest memories were of those revival days when the Spirit of God swept through Cambridge. Sometimes there were meetings of 800 or more students, but every day there were prayer meetings and so many students were swept into the Kingdom of God. In my final term, Jackie Pullinger from Hong Kong preached for several days in my church and so many of the very conservative evangelical students in the Christian Union found their way out to my church and were "baptized in the Spirit". It was a landmark moment, not only for the Cambridge Christian Union (CICCU) and Cambridge Missions, but also for the future of the Christian faith across the UK and beyond. God has His moments, and this was one of them.

I've come to know Revd David MacInnes, the Cambridge Mission evangelist, quite well since that time. Apparently he nearly cancelled the Student Mission as he felt such an onslaught of mental confusion:

hell was obviously threatened by what was about to take place. It was during that five-day mission that about 150 students surrendered to God's plan for their lives, many of whom are now significant leaders, even bishops, in the Anglican church. Indirectly one of these students then helped the current Archbishop of Canterbury to come to faith; others impacted were people like Nicky Gumbel, who birthed the Alpha course; Ken Costa, a leading financier in the City of London and a core supporter of Alpha; Nicky and Sila Lee of The Marriage Course, together with many others who made an impact in the Christian world. Unknowingly I was being birthed spiritually in an era of intense revival significance and this would continue to fuel the fire of my future passion to serve the purposes of God.

5

GERMAN ENCOUNTERS

From the hothouse atmosphere of Cambridge revival, I was then immersed back into the frigid spiritual waters of my Regiment in Celle, North Germany. There were no committed Christians that I could find, so I joined a little German Elim Church led by an 84-year-old revivalist called Herman Dittert. His wife apparently had been the Sunday School teacher of a promising young evangelist called Reinhard Bonnke! What a privilege to be impacted by a man who, like Charles Finney, saw whole communities in his youth come under deep conviction and weeping. My German certainly became more fluent, but deep down I was desperate for English-speaking fellowship. God was about to blow my mind with four separate encounters.

I had heard that Bob Humburg from Christ for the Nations, had just planted a new Bible School in Wolfenbüttel, close to the East German border. I took some leave and was soon sitting in their conference room listening to stories of God's healing power: in one of the sessions, suddenly that divine presence, which I recognized from the encounter in Cambridge, flooded into the room.

The young man next to me shouted out as the fire of God burned through his head: he shouted out, "God's healed me! I had several terminal brain tumours and I believe the fire of God has just burnt them away!" (He was later to confirm, with medical reports, that these tumours had totally disappeared.) What was even more mind-blowing for me, was that one of the girls I had noticed on arrival, whose legs, body and face were distorted, jumped out of her seat and ran around the building! God had totally realigned her disabled legs, and to me it seemed that her whole face and body were transformed. What a Big God! He was deliberately expanding my small English view of Him.

After several months, my hunger for English fellowship returned and I heard that the American Forces were having a weekend of Christian meetings in Nuremberg in the south of Germany. I just jumped in my car and prayed a naïve child-like prayer: "Father, I have no idea where the conference is: please help me find it. Oh, and I need a bed for the night!"

As I was driving into the expansive city of Nuremberg, I kept my eyes open. Suddenly one of my tyres burst: I parked up and ran across to a hotel opposite, only to discover that this was the hotel where the delegates to the conference were staying! Remarkably, when I returned to my car, there were two men standing there asking if they could help me change my spare wheel! It was only years later that I realized that God had probably sent some angels to help – having burst my tyre in the first place!

God moved so powerfully that day and I was deeply touched. As the final session concluded, I waited outside the conference building, hoping that someone would offer me a bed for the night. No one came. As I began to walk away a little disappointed, suddenly a short guy began running towards me simply saying, "The Holy Spirit's just sent me back to collect you." "Wow! That's cool!", I thought to myself.

I had no idea God did this stuff. Back at their home, I discovered a sad truth, that this man was a Canadian missionary whose wife had become deeply offended by God due to her dad's tragic death in an industrial accident. They both felt very alone, ineffective, and forgotten.

They quizzed me at length about how on earth a British Army Officer like me had become a believer. So, as I told them the whole story of how God had pursued me up to a little Eskimo village in northern Canada called Tuytoyaktuk, tears started rolling down their cheeks. "You have no idea what this means to us", the man said, "I was a Canadian missionary up in Tuk! Maybe those Eskimos you saw were ones that I led to the Lord!" Wow! He is an even bigger God, I realized!

About a year later, I took some leave and drove down to the Youth With A Mission base in Schloss Hurlach, near Augsburg, in the deep south of Germany. I had met Phil Hampe, the YWAM Director for Ministry to the Armed Forces, in one of those God-incidents (actually in the loo!) during the conference in Nuremberg. Phil and his wife, Sondra, ministered to me at a deeper level than ever before. None of us was expecting the outpouring of God's Spirit which happened that week: amongst the small group of about thirty YWAM students, there was a sense of depression: one by one they stood up and confessed that they didn't know why they were feeling so isolated and distant from God, and so hardened in their emotions.

It was as a young girl confessed that she hadn't cried in prayer for months, and felt so far from God, that it happened: suddenly the heavy weight of God's glory flooded into the room, and each of us was physically thrown off our seats as the weight of His presence pressed us to the floor. God had just burst into the room! This is the only time in my life that I audibly heard God's voice. It was not a condemning tone but almost pleading, imploring me to believe how much He loved me. These experiences of God ruined me for life and I knew that I could never be satisfied with mere outward forms of religious duty and just attending church. I had just met God. He loved me, and He had a plan for my whole life! In my next regiment I was required to lead the Regimental Cross-Country Ski Team for four months each year. It was an idyllic existence but yet, deep down, my hunger and passion for God was still burning. I remember returning from winning the Army Ski Championships but hungry for more, so I decided to take time each evening just to wait on God in the little army chapel.

However, as the months rolled by, rather than letting this tangible experience of God hold me, I began to become introspective and let my old doubts and insecurities resurface again. One evening I saw that a white dove had become trapped in the chapel, but each day as I tried to catch it and set it free, it just flapped its way up to the rafters and then landed somewhere else exhausted. It took a few days for the dove to become so weak that it couldn't flutter away: it lay there panting its last breaths. I gently put my hands around it and walked it to the door: as I released it and threw it into the air, into freedom, God spoke to me! "That's exactly what you have been doing to me. Every time I try to put my hands on you to harness you, you just flap away saying, 'I can do it, I can do it!', and you end up depressed and exhausted by your own efforts. It's time for you to surrender to my love and let me take hold of you."

Just after this, I was sent down to Reindahlen in the south of Germany on a training course. Inside me was a raw longing for God, and yet a deep frustration that he would not talk to me. As I was walking down the road one day, a young Ghanaian man whom I'd never met before, came up to me and said: "God's sent me to you because He's desperate to get through to you!"

In my frustration, it's a wonder I didn't punch this guy! He asked me to follow him back to his room where he explained himself: "God showed me that you've been praying and praying and digging yourself into a tight spot with a wall of unbelief getting thicker and thicker. You need to understand that God doesn't answer just 'prayer' – He answers 'prayers of faith'. Faith comes by hearing God speak to you as you read His Word. I want you to go back and approach the Bible as if you were a child: take Psalm 23 and begin to thank God all day long as you read through the Psalm. Don't beg, just thank Him that He's your shepherd and that he will lead you and restore your soul. Keep thanking him until you feel faith comes."

Back in my regiment I began to repeat this Psalm, engaging my spirit again and again, all day long. It took three days for the concrete wall of unbelief to crumble: I will never forget the evening in the chapel when I was pacing round as usual, rehearsing Psalm 23: "Thank you, Father, that you are my Shepherd. You're never going to let me down. Thank you that you'll walk me through some horrific things, but I will never have to fear". I droned on an on with little emotional feeling or conviction.

Suddenly I tangibly felt faith come. I began to leap and jump and run around the chapel: "Yes! Yes! Yes! I know you are my Shepherd! What a God! Amazing! I will never doubt you again." Ever since that moment, prayer has been a different world to me – hearing God speak to me from his Word and then thanking Him for what He's promised. The days of pleading in unbelief were over.

These four encounters with God radically changed my whole perception and perspective about the God who had saved me. I now knew beyond doubt that He was a big, big God, much bigger than anything I had ever dreamed of. His planning department was mind-blowing, being able to arrange for people to speak His word to me, connect me to people whom I needed to meet – on a global scale – and a God who would forever presence Himself to me and audibly speak to me.

It was time now for the strongholds inside me to be challenged: the fear of man and the stubborn independence needed to be blasted out of the way to make way for God's higher purpose. The years in Germany were over and I was beginning to be trained to step into the Northern Ireland crisis with my regiment. Once again, the scene was being set by God for some major heart surgery. This next season was triggered by a clear word from God that it was time to leave the Army and serve him full-time. Sadly, my military heritage and sense of pride about coming from generations of distinguished army officers, woven with my fear of family pressure and reputation, caused me to ignore and refuse God's call.

6

IRISH SHOWDOWN

The scene for a showdown with God was being set. The painful historic religious wounds in Northern Ireland had flared into a sectarian conflict which was beyond reason. I soon found myself, together with the majority of the British Army, involved in an annual schedule of one month's intense training, followed by four months' active service in Northern Ireland.

My first tour was divided in two parts: first guarding the high security prison which was nicknamed The Maze in Long Kesh, Hillsborough, before then moving across to Londonderry on the north coast. I arrived at the Maze Prison just as the inmates started what became known as "the Dirty Protest", where men from the IRA would smear their excreta all over the walls of their cells and often refused to wear clothes. The situation was in deadlock but Christians began to pray. So I found myself every lunch time on my face before God, praying together with the Christian prison wardens, seeking God for answers.

Remarkably God began to move, and quite a few convicted terrorists became believers during that time. I remember one little 70-year-old lady, Gladys Blackburn, who prayed with us during the lunch breaks. She was courageous and after prayer she would then walk around these cells filled with men who were like wild animals: it was unbelievable how they became as meek as lambs as she entered, risking her life. She carried such a presence and love of God that their demonic nature was tamed, and they would listen to her talking about God's love and plans for their lives.

In my off-duty moments, I would go up to the Robinson's farm on the hill beyond the prison and would pray with the family for a move of God. Many years later, I discovered that God had moved, and the Hillsborough Elim church was built, which began the annual Hillsborough Bible Week Camp which for years became the gathering point for spirit-filled believers across Northern Ireland.

My tour in Londonderry began with the most enormous bomb exploding in the centre of the city, on the first day I arrived: there was so much devastation! In my off-duty hours, I travelled around the beautiful north coast in a little Mini car, dressed in civilian clothes, with a loaded pistol hidden in the glove compartment. Fortunately, I was never challenged and never had to use the pistol. It was so unreal, travelling amongst such beauty, and yet in the midst of such danger and national unrest. With my southern Irish background, I found it deeply moving to see my own people being torn apart.

A year later, having told God that there was no way that I could leave the Army to serve him, I found myself back in Northern Ireland, but this time in the area of Armagh which we called "Bandit Country". During the training for this tour, I was appointed as the Operations Officer, to oversee all the daily patrols both in vehicles and on foot. I was the Battery Captain, but my Battery Commander was a man who absolutely hated my Christian faith and made life impossible for me. My internal desire to please him went into overdrive, and I stressed myself daily to the point of exhaustion: there was no pleasing him. As we flew from Germany to Armagh, he announced to me that he was taking over my role and demoting me to the role of Watchkeeper in the Operations Room, monitoring everything that happened in the patrols.

Naïvely I thought that because I was a believer, all my soldiers would be kept safe from the guerilla-style of terrorist activity all around us. Within the first week, I had lost four of my soldiers, who were blown to pieces by a remote-controlled land mine, which was triggered by some cowardly IRA terrorists hiding in a wood close to the road. As I picked up the news in the Operations Room, my whole world exploded internally.

I knew that I had disobeyed God about leaving the Army, so I felt that I was the "Jonah" who was directly responsible for their deaths. I felt intense shame and guilt, feeling that I had not only failed my Commanding Officer again, but had also failed my own military father, the wives and girlfriends of all these soldiers – and God too. Of course, the truth was that their deaths had nothing to do with me or with what I had done, but I internalized all the pain, shame and guilt and tormented myself with these thoughts. We immediately sent a team out to collect the fragments of their bodies, and then I had to contact all their next of kin and inform them of the tragedy. I was traumatized.

I woke up the next morning and discovered that my internal emotional and spiritual circuitry had totally blown a fuse: I was incapacitated and began to descend rapidly into a form of PTSD (Post Traumatic Stress Disorder). I was unable to talk to my soldiers without crippling panic attacks and unable to eat in front of my fellow officers without shaking uncontrollably. Sadly, PTSD was unrecognized at that time, and only discovered a couple of years later. So I was not referred to any doctor, but just hauled up in front of my Commanding Officer and told that my behaviour was unacceptable, and I would have to leave the Army.

God was about to challenge the stronghold of the fear of man that was crippling me. Although discharged from the Army, I was not allowed to leave my position immediately. So, in order to survive, I decided I needed to pray and take communion in my room just by myself. This was no religious ritual, but a cry for help. As I pleaded with God on the floor, I took a little bit of bread and a sip of blackcurrant juice every morning saying, "God, I know I've failed you and disobeyed you, but please do not let me go. You have made a covenant contract with me and I need your help. I cannot end up as a broken wreck with all these panic attacks."

Initially nothing seemed to change, but in desperation I persisted with this daily routine of breaking bread for about 6 weeks (somehow God loves 40 days!). As I was breaking bread on one of these final days, God gave me such a powerful revelation of the Cross, it changed my life forever. It was a landmark moment. I suddenly saw how I could move, by faith, from one side of the Cross where I lived in all my fear, over to the other side of the Cross where Jesus had not only delivered me from all fear, but had also clothed me with a new mantle of boldness and the gift of faith.

In an instant I was delivered from a spirit of fear, but it took about eighteen months for this truth to totally manifest in the way I thought and lived. The Bible clearly says that we "work out our salvation from the inside", and that is exactly what happened: the little seed of faith began to grow and fill every part of my being, and within eighteen months I was back to full mental health. As I left Ireland, I remember God clearly spoke to me: "If you will humble yourself under my hand, and under the Cross, I will totally deliver you and will transform your life and ministry."

Having been honourably discharged from the Army, I was welcomed back to my parents' home where, to my surprise, I was not treated as a failure, but instead I was loved unconditionally and encouraged in my recovery. I did however take three days away in a caravan to seek God, and during that time He spoke to me about the seed of fear that had been sown into my life, and He told me that He wanted to dynamite the dam that I had built around my heart and emotions. As I asked Him to forgive me, a new day dawned and the dam, which had sealed my heart and emotions, began to burst.

Over the coming weeks I visited my pastor, Alan Vincent, who regularly prayed for me: it was at one of these visits that one of his friends, John Greenlees, happened to be with him. As John shook my hand, I could see something happened between us. As he sat down he said: "I believe God has just spoken to me and He wants me to take you on as a trainee recruitment consultant, working with me in Executive Resources International (ERI). I know you are still in recovery, but I believe this period with me will be a time of healing and will restore your confidence to talk to people without panic attacks".

Over the next eighteen months, John taught me everything he knew and together we began to recruit project management teams for Arabic construction companies in Saudi Arabia and the Gulf. I watched how John would daily lay out the recruitment needs on the table and ask God to give us the right people to fill these vacancies. Miraculously, God would send exactly the right person to us to fill each vacancy and as we continued this practice of allowing Jesus to be our Senior Partner, our little department in ERI became by far the most financially successful department. Those months taught me how to live by faith.

John and I had talked about setting up our own company to focus just on construction personnel. Then suddenly one day, during a routine medical check-up, John had a heart attack and died. I was devastated but, in memory of John, I made plans to set up the company we had talked about.

Miraculously, shortly after deciding to step out in faith to form this new company, I met with a client called Bill Benko from Kuwait Piling Company. I had noticed a Christian fish sign on his lapel, so I shared my vision to set up a Christian recruitment company in the construction field which would be used to fund a Christian school. Immediately Bill offered to fund the whole start-up and insisted that he trusted me to steward the money safely. "God is my accountant", he said, "just report to Him." I have never seen Bill since, though I have often longed to tell him what God did with his investment. His investment was the first financial seed into my life.

How remarkable that God could restore me in such a short time, and then launch me out as a company director. The sad fact is that, initially, I did it my way and so I was heading for some more dealings with God – more about this in chapter 8. But first let me share with you how God surprised me with love!

7

SURPRISED BY LOVE!

On one of my trips home to visit my parents, while still serving in the Army, I had become so frustrated with my local church service that I decided just to walk and pray. I ended up walking to the next village of Bedmond and, as I walked through, I heard the most angelic singing coming from a little tin roof colonial style chapel. Curious, I went to investigate, but I was spotted by the lady at the door who quickly ushered me to a seat at the back of this church. Since my conversion at Cambridge, I had been desperate for spirit-filled worship and a sense of the presence of God. The atmosphere was overwhelming: God was there! At the end, the lady at the door asked my name and I quickly rushed off.

It was perhaps a year later that I found myself back from Germany on leave again, and I rushed back to that church to discover more of what God was doing. To my amazement, I was greeted by my name! The same lady at the door hugged me and remembered my name. I felt so at home, and afterwards asked if I could have some time with the pastor, Alan Vincent. The following week, I drove over to his house and discovered his 16-year-old daughter, Rachel, was studying in the garden for her exams: I rather rudely threw her books off the chair in the garden, patted her on the head, wishing her well for her exams, and took the chair to go and sit with her dad. It was "hate at first sight"! This patronizing army officer just breezing into the garden, disturbing her revision, and stealing her chair to talk with her dad!

I soon had to return to my unit in Germany and wrote to the church requesting if someone could write to me regularly and send me the tape messages from the Pastor's teaching series. To my amazement I soon received a letter from his daughter, Rachel, with the tape. Apparently, one of the house group leaders had asked if there was anyone who liked writing letters. Rachel volunteered as she had been a prolific letter writer while at boarding school in India. However, she did not know that she was being asked to write to this rude, patronizing British army officer who was 10 years older than her! Once she had volunteered, her sense of duty meant it was too late to back out. God was having a laugh! We both found that whenever either of us wrote and shared what we had been reading, it was exactly the same passage that the other one was reading: the revelation that Rachel was having from the Word was uncanny. She was reading exactly what I read but was seeing a complementary revelation that I had not seen.

Rachel's father invited me that summer to join the whole church camping together at the Dales Bible Week. Just the year before, at the same camp, Rachel had a visitation of angels after she prayed for some friends to be filled with the Holy Spirit. She found it hard to describe but she saw a whole company of angels breaking through above her and coming down to a place just above her head. It was widely documented that the angels had broken into that camp, with many reported sightings, but it was always the youth and children who saw them, and not the adults: a lost child was returned to his parents by an angel, and, at night, angels were heard singing in the main venue! It was so loud that some of the local residents around the camp complained, and they were told their complaint had been sent to "higher authorities"! That year had also been a turning point for Rachel as she stood up at the end of one meeting determined to dedicate her life to God for His exclusive service. She had decided she wanted to live a Kingdom life, totally given to God.

Having heard all these stories, I was eager to accept Rachel's dad's invitation and went willingly to the Dales Bible Week with the church. Once I arrived, I was asked if I could teach Rachel to drive (being an Army Driving Examiner). At the end of the Bible Week, making the most of the opportunity for further driving practice, Rachel drove all the way back to Kings Langley and we talked all the way. A bond was being forged.

Rachel's parents had been missionaries in Bombay, India. Rachel spent her childhood at a very conservative boarding school called Hebron High School, a thousand miles from home, south of Bombay in the Nilgiri hills. She had been baptized in the Spirit at the age of ten through Arthur Wallis's ministry, and then began to pray for many other girls at her school too. For several years these girls would get up every morning at 6 am and go up to the top hockey pitch to pray for India.

As these girls wrote home, delighted about their new spiritual faith, concerned parents and the conservative staff began to consider their response. It was quickly decided that Rachel was an unhelpful influence and should be isolated from the other girls. One member of staff even labeled her as the devil's child and advised that she should sleep separately from her friends. School was not a happy place and she was severely bullied for her faith. In the end it was advised that she should be removed for being a disruptive influence in the school and so, at the age of fifteen, she was sent home to the UK. She lived with guardians for one year in Frimley until her parents could extricate themselves from India and return to make home back in England. This left Rachel feeling deeply wounded and rejected.

I had first met Rachel soon after her parents had returned from India, when they had established Bedmond Chapel as a little revival centre. But I found myself being strangely drawn to this fascinating teenager and, as I was ten years older than her, I never imagined that there would be any romantic connection between us. I used to naïvely offer to walk the pastor's dog and would take Rachel along: we would talk for hours and we both found a fascinating connection in the Spirit. She shared that her dream was to be a medical doctor in Shining Hospital Green Pastures, in Pokhara, Nepal. She wanted to work amongst the leprosy-affected in the hospital there.

On one of her youth trips away to Wales, God showed Rachel a picture of a jigsaw puzzle as she was praying about her future. As the pieces of this puzzle all came together in this prophetic picture, she realized that there was a significant piece missing. When she prayed about the missing piece God spoke to her that this was her husband. At this time, we were just beginning to become friends and she wondered deep down if it was God's plan for us to be married.

Rachel's mum had been praying against this alliance as she was concerned and saw the potential disaster of me courting her innocent daughter. One day she confronted me and said that she noticed that I got on so well with other people's wives and that it was time that I found my own! Little was she to know that it would be her own daughter! However, as she was coming down the stairs one day, she heard God tell her to stop praying against me because I was going to be her son-in-law, and that I would be an "angel" to the Church!

God had more faith in me than I did! I was soon to become embroiled in all the trauma of Northern Ireland. As my mental health took a nose-dive due to the Post Traumatic Stress Disorder, I told Rachel that I would not be seeing her anymore, as I did not want her to be damaged by watching me going through the terrible meltdowns and panic attacks that I had just entered. I said that we should stop writing all letters and there should be no further contact.

Several months later I suddenly realized how much I missed Rachel, so I wrote to her a simple letter of friendship, signing it from "your brother in Christ". I was shocked when this letter was returned to me as "Return to Sender – Person unknown": I later discovered that when Rachel received this letter without any explanation, she had steamed it open, been hurt by the distant non-committal tone, and decided to send it back seemingly unopened! She was not prepared to get hurt again. As I sat crying on my military bed in "the bandit country" of Armagh, I realized that, whether I liked it or not, this young girl had become a part of my life and I loved her! Our lives had already become deeply entwined, and I longed to be together with her. This relationship was becoming so complex for me.

It must have been about six months later, still without any contact with Rachel, that I was praying one night. As I prayed, God encouraged me with a picture: I saw myself walking along a woodland path towards a bright light; I suddenly became aware of a girl walking beside me and I simply reached out, took her hand, and continued walking. This dream was exactly what was about to happen.

My army chaplain and his wife had become close friends with me and I had also formed a bond with their four kids. These growing teenagers then persuaded me to attend the New Forest Bible week with them. Unfortunately, I needed to arrive a day after the setup, so the children had already made camp for us, having been given a space with one of the churches. On my arrival, all four kids ran up to me and, with great excitement, recounted their story from the previous day. The youngest, Alistair, had celebrated his 13th birthday on the campsite the day before. As soon as their adopted church discovered it was Alistair's birthday, they decided to pray for him and give him a birthday blessing. A girl called Rachel from this church had prayed with the birthday boy, and as a result he was baptized in the Spirit! So a friendship had been formed with the young people of this church and these four kids and they had arranged a walk in the woods for today. These kids were so excited and insisted that I should now come and join this group for a walk and meet everyone.

What a shock when we met each other! That day, as we walked through the woods together, I became aware of Rachel close at my side: we joined hands and continued to walk side by side. Of course, the matchmaker of heaven had engineered all this, and we found ourselves being thrown together, with the kids constantly making very forward remarks about what we really felt about each other. On the first evening, Arthur Wallis decided to just read the whole of Hebrews instead of preaching. As the Word flowed over my Spirit, God spoke to me and told me that I was to make a covenant with Rachel that day, and give myself to her, even though I was still struggling with my confidence and emotions.

Unbeknown to me, Rachel was sitting in another part of the conference tent. She felt during the reading that, despite her renewed feelings, and the picture that God had given her about me being her possible future husband, she had to be prepared to let me go and choose God first. She wept as she finally told God that she was ready to do anything He asked and obey him. It sounds clichéd, but after the service I headed out of the tent and, suddenly, in front of me, I saw a girl trip over the large tent peg and guy ropes, and I reached out and just managed to catch her before she fell head first into the mud. It was Rachel! Shocked, we looked at each other, and then both blurted out at the same time, "I've got something I must talk to you about!"

We must have talked until 3am and, by the time we both went to bed, I had made it totally clear that my life was hers. For me it was an act of obedience, as the recent trauma had completely sealed up all my emotions and I was unable to trust my feelings. Although I knew that Rachel was God's perfect partner for me, I struggled to connect with my feelings. A few weeks later, we were back at home, and again Rachel and I were walking. After a long walk, I will never forget, as we turned to walk down Love Lane near the Kings Langley Common, God suddenly dropped a seed of tangible love into my heart and I began to cry. It was the first time in my memory that I had actually been able to feel any emotion. The concrete around my heart was beginning to yield.

I was utterly surprised by love and, within days, that seed grew and we were overwhelmed with love for each other and began to talk at every spare moment about our future lives together. We really knew each other deeply even before we were married: so much so that, to my shame, I introduced her as my fiancée at the Army Christian Union Conference at High Leigh Conference Centre before I had even proposed. It was to be a source of many future disputes!

We planned our wedding for the 11th July 1981, the following summer, and then proceeded to step out in faith to buy a house. Things went so fast that we very soon had purchased and decorated our new home and, although we had printed the most beautiful wedding invites in India for the July date, it seemed far too long to wait! So we quickly adjusted the date and sent out the same invites with a sticker across the envelope: "Stop Press! Changed date! March 21st or you'll be late. Same time, same place! Sorry! Couldn't wait!"

Amazingly, everyone got the message and we had the most moving wedding. We did however make a mental note to ensure that Rachel did not get pregnant straight away, to remove any grounds of suspicion concerning the rushed wedding from any concerned friends or relatives!

Okay – confession time! I had planned the most beautiful honeymoon in a cottage in the Wordsworth country of the Lake District. Thankfully, Rachel was just too inquisitive about all the arrangements, and managed to sneak a look at the booking forms for this romantic cottage. "You've got to be joking!", she shrieked, "This place looks gorgeous but you didn't read the small-print! It is only furnished with bunk beds!" I am so thankful for my inquisitive Rachel! Fortunately, her dad came to the rescue and we very soon cancelled the cottage and spent our honeymoon in his large caravan-home up above lake Windermere. We started married life surrounded by fields of daffodils, with the idyllic lake and mountain views.

Over 20 years later, long married, I decided it was time to rectify my youthful negligence of never proposing to Rachel. One weekend, Rachel was away leading a women's conference at that same High Leigh Conference Centre where I had prematurely introduced her as my "fiancée": I secretly drove down to the conference centre and, as she was preaching, I snuck in the back door with the biggest bouquet of flowers I could order! I got down on my knees on the platform in front of 200 women and pleaded with her to marry me! Amidst all the sighs from the ladies, all I could get from Rachel was, "I will think about it!"

8

KOREAN FAITH

Rachel was never attracted to the army uniform as she never actually saw me in it. As I already shared, we had married quickly, and both began working in London. I had left the army and had become a business consultant, recruiting construction project teams for Saudi Arabia and the Gulf. Rachel's working world was totally different to mine: she had graduated from university and was working at St Bartholomew's Hospital where she was now a clinical research scientist specializing in the detection of hormones. Today she playfully remarks that this skill is still helpful when needing to understand the competitive male testosterone manifesting in a room! As a research scientist she loved working with a team, pushing the frontiers of diagnostic medicine, and developing assays that would give a quicker or more efficient result from pregnancy testing to hormone concentrations.

On one occasion, her team had reached an impasse with the development of a new pregnancy test. She was reminded about her dad's earlier career as a research chemist with Kodak and how he had received blue prints of inventions direct from God. Now Rachel was challenged to do the same. So she asked to take three days as reading and study leave, but really it was three days to seek God for the key to the breakthrough. As she prayed, God showed her the way she could change the process to get through this impasse. However, on her return, her professor told her categorically that this idea made no sense scientifically but she pleaded with him to trust her and asked for the best grade of chemicals to do her experiment. Of course, God knew the way through this scientific blockage and the experiment produced a breakthrough which we now take for granted every time we do a pregnancy test.

Although she was extremely busy, Rachel watched the extraordinary way in which God then provided the funds for me to start the new recruitment business after my friend died but, being a very wise and prophetic wife, she warned me not to do it in my way. Unfortunately, my pride and independence overruled her advice, and I set up my new company, naïvely expecting my old company's blessing. The new company took off and within a few weeks I was in Seoul, Korea, talking with Christian Korean construction directors who worked in the Middle East on massive projects that needed project management teams.

Based in Korea, Dr. Cho Yonghi's church was the largest church in the world: my mother-in-law had spent some time over in Seoul interviewing Dr Cho and had then written a powerful book called "God can do it here!" to encourage English Christians to move in faith for church growth. Having found that my main client was a member of this church, I excitedly got up early to attend the church. When I arrived at 7am on Sunday morning, I was shocked to see that there were already 10,000 people coming out from the earlier service, as another 10,000 made their way in. I was overwhelmed by the vastness of the vision, knowing that hundreds of thousands of people called this place their church.

My old company had become aware of my travel plans through our travel agent and as soon as I flew out of England, they applied for a Court Injunction to block my new company from trading. I received this news from Rachel as I woke up the next day in Seoul. "Darling, we are in the High Court in London! We are being sued for everything we own. What do I do?" My ego trip crashed, and I came face to face with reality.

As I got up that morning, I just cried out to God. "Father, I'm so sorry I did it my way. I've totally messed up. What should I do? Should I persevere and fight this, or should I just give in and yield to the demands of my previous company?" I had no idea what to do. My previous company was claiming that I had taken their clients and information from the company files and was now trading with this information, imitating my old company. Of course, none of this was true, but since I was in Korea and we were still a single man company, there was no one else in the UK and the case was due in court the following week.

But I had underestimated my precious wife who, aged just 22, took the injunction papers, mimicked their legal language and went to represent me. The opposing party's solicitors were shocked when she turned up in court on the Monday and stood up to defend me. "She has no legal right to do this, as she is only a wife and the injunction was taken out against the company", they complained to the Judge. "Oh yes, I have!", Rachel responded, "I have not come as Gordon's wife but I am legally the Company Secretary and so acting on behalf of the company." Her wedding vows, "for better, or worse; for richer, or poorer", became very relevant that day as she stood on our third wedding anniversary in the courtroom and managed single-handedly to stay the injunction and win the right to postpone the hearing until I returned and retained a solicitor.

Over in Korea, God was about to answer my heart's cry in an

extraordinary way. I still had a long list of clients to visit so I headed off into the teaming millions on the streets of Seoul. As I was crossing a footbridge, I became aware of a group of European nuns who were coming towards me. Suddenly one of them reached her hand out to me and said, in her strong German accent, "We have the Word of God for you today!" She reached out and put a bookmark in my hand: to my amazement it said, "Stand firm and persevere! For I know the trouble you have entered today, and I have already chosen the time when I will come to your rescue." I was stunned! How on earth could God answer me so exactly within a matter of hours after my prayer?

I poured out my troubles to my next client on the list who was also a member of this Korean church. "You need to go up to Prayer Mountain", he said. "That is where everyone goes to pray when they are facing problems. You will definitely hear God up there and you will know what to do." I caught the bus that afternoon up to Prayer Mountain and could not believe my eyes as I saw thousands of people praying all around me. The prayer leader for English speakers took me up to the Prayer Grottos and opened the door of a tiny cave, which was not big enough to stand in so I had to kneel immediately, ushered me into this space and then he left me to pray like that all night. He said, "Pray, Pray, Pray! God will speak to you, and I will come and find you in the morning."

I could hear people all around me in other caves, crying out to God and weeping, but had no idea how to pray about this issue. I had learnt to pray in Germany but this was different: suddenly I felt a wave of God's Spirit come on me, and I was immersed in a spirit of prayer for the first time in my life. It poured through me and I literally prayed all night. By dawn, God had spoken to me about three things: firstly, I would win the court case; secondly, the other company would cease to trade; and thirdly, I would eventually be reconciled with the director of my old company.

It actually took two years to win the court case and seven years before the other company stopped trading. Eight years later I managed to talk with my ex-director and was reconciled. Those years of walking in faith, knowing that God had spoken clearly to me, shaped my life for the future. I learnt my foundational lessons of faith from the cut and thrust of the business world, not in Church or on the mission field. I am eternally grateful that God allowed me to catch "the spirit of prayer" from what was probably the most powerful strategic prayer centre in the world at that time.

Back in the UK, we changed the name of our company and for the next few years I became extremely busy, recruiting for all kinds of projects around the Middle East. I don't know why, but I was constantly being drawn towards this area of the world, and I found it fascinating to be working in Saudi Arabia, Bahrain, Kuwait and the Gulf region. I remember one time recruiting a top engineering Quantity Surveyor for the construction of the Mosul Dam in North Iraq. I knew that the Iran-Iraq war was still inflamed but I risked flying into Baghdad and drove up to Mosul to see the directors of this massive project. There was no danger up north, as the whole war effort was down in the south.

Once the business was completed, I drove back to Baghdad to fly home to the UK, and to my horror was informed that the airport had just been closed due to the war alert! My only option to get home was to hire a friendly taxi driver and make it worth his while to drive me all the way down through the war zone until we arrived safely in Kuwait from where I was able to fly home safely. This taxi driver came from southern Iraq so he invited me to sleep with his family overnight while on our adventurous journey. Looking back on this time, it is a wonder that I am still alive to tell the tale. Fortunately, the Iraqi people had not yet been soured against the British and I was met with friendship and hospitality throughout the journey.

Even though I had been incredibly independent and made mistakes, nothing is ever wasted with God: during these years of directing my small recruitment consultancy, I learned so many lessons of faith. God was slowly bringing me to a place of surrender and teaching me to trust Him in every aspect of my life. I was not there yet but I was certainly progressing on this pathway of God's dealings.

Despite our hectic professional lives at the time, both Rachel and I were passionate about our involvement in our local church. We belonged to Garston Church, one of the five churches which had grown from the move of God started by Rachel's father. Just six months after we married, we were asked to lead a connect group, as well as being closely involved with shaping the church youth group. Our house group consisted of five young people who had just come out of a cult, three young men who were struggling with their sexual identity and life's purpose, a returned missionary who felt a failure and others, who along with us, were also complex! God told us just to give ourselves unconditionally to these people and so we broke bread everytime we met and prayed for each other. The group doubled in six months: our friends from the cult were baptized in the Spirit and two of them later became leaders of significant churches. Those who had battled with their identity fell in love, got married and had kids, another set up a national ministry to help young men with their sexuality, and the ex-missionary set up the most effective charity to reach the homeless and addicted in our town.

We were beginning to see the impact of God working through ordinary harnessed surrendered lives. God was preparing us so that we would be ready to surrender to a major call on our lives. This would require both of us to surrender our careers and follow His leading to work unpaid in Africa and Asia for many years. We were totally unaware of this and there were still more challenges to come. My stubborn streak needed further God confrontations!

9

THE AFRICA CALL

What a joy it was that our daughter, Nicola, was born on my birthday on April 27th, 1984. Within a few months we bravely decided that we would go with our church to the Downs Bible Week. This summer tradition was more affectionately known as "Drowns Bible Week" by those who attended due to the fact that it always rained, and with everyone living in tents on the muddy farming fields, people usually spent the week trying to keep dry and their tents from flooding! We must have been mad to go camping with our 3-month-old baby!

Since this was our holiday time we chose several books to take with us to read including one called "Plundering Hell to Populate Heaven." This book had caught Rachel's attention and was a story about a man called Reinhard Bonnke in South Africa and about how God called him to build the world's largest tent, seating 34,000 people, for his massive Gospel Crusades. Rachel had already read this book and had begun to tell me about the stories of miracles and faith. As I began to read it now, I felt a strange sensation and actually felt God impress on me that we would work with this man in Africa. Once I had finished the book, I then asked Rachel if she had sensed anything, without telling her what I felt, and was totally shocked when she instantly responded and said, "I believe God wants us to work with him!"

Shortly after this, Rachel had a dream: she dreamt that Reinhard Bonnke had come to speak in the UK and that we were in the meeting with our whole youth group to hear him. As the dream continued, she saw a large stage with Rachel and I standing down at the front of this stage, asking Reinhard to pray over a handkerchief which we wanted to take and lay on a close friend who was at home, terminally ill with cancer. Within weeks, exactly that had happened: Bonnke came to Birmingham and we took our whole youth group and they were deeply impacted. As Reinhard preached passionately, he suddenly paused and said, "I believe that some of you in this meeting tonight will launch out into the deep and join me in Africa." As we stood at the front, pressing up against this stage that Rachel recognized from her dream, we felt the impact of this call to Africa and wondered what our next step would be. Reinhard Bonnke did pray over a handkerchief for our friend Mandy, who was dying of cancer, who had a baby just Nicola's age, and we returned home shaken, knowing we had heard a call to Africa.

After the impact of our time in Birmingham I was still trying to understand this stirring in our hearts for Africa. So imagine our shock when, on the following Sunday morning, in our own church, Jim, one of our friends from our connect group, stood up to share a word that he had received and made this bold statement – "Launch out into the deep… and cut all your ties!" We had never heard Jim share so boldly and it convicted us. It couldn't have been a clearer confirmation for me that God was calling us.

Then we heard that Reinhard Bonnke was finishing his UK tour with a final service in Kensington Temple, London, that very Sunday evening. So Rachel and I rushed down to London to hear him, carrying little Nicola with us. In the middle of his preaching, he suddenly stopped and pointed down to where we were sitting and said, "I believe there are even people sitting right here tonight, who will join me on this 'Crusade Caravan Trail' from Capetown to Cairo." We both knew immediately that it was a confirmation of God's call for us to serve Him in Africa.

Although the church came to faith and prayed tirelessly for Mandy to be healed, she sadly died. This was an intensely confusing moment, as we had so believed for life. After she had died, we even prayed over her dead body, and during this time Rachel's father received a very strong word from God that, because Mandy had died while the church was in faith for her to live, He was going to give us a harvest of one hundred lives who would be miraculously rescued from death. Over the following years, Rachel's dad saw so many miracles but little did he know that his own daughter would be one of these lives that would fulfil this prophecy!

In September 1984, with Nicola only five months old, I took six weeks off from work and we flew out to Harare, Zimbabwe, to explore this call as a family. We stayed in the YWAM house on Cork Road and worked as volunteers with the Christ for all Nations (CfaN) team in the prayer tent, deliverance area, and the offices helping with the follow-up after each evening crusade meeting. Deep inside I was wrestling with the call of God. I was not sure I wanted to permanently relocate to Africa and serve God as a missionary here. My argument was surely we could just catch this revival fire of prayer and evangelism, with the demonstration of extraordinary miracles, and just take it back to the UK.

This time in Harare was our first introduction to real intercession led by Suzette Hattingh. Every night the prayer room became the generator of power for what then manifested in the meeting as Reinhard Bonnke preached. We were amazed as whatever we prayed in that intercession room seemed to immediately happen later in the service. I will never forget how God spoke to us all in the prayer tent about his desire to heal all the cripples this particular night. Then the hundreds of intercessors packed in this room began to warfare and cry out for a spirit of healing to release the cripples, just like a calf from the stall. Later, as we walked back into the crusade meeting, we saw tens of thousands of people listening intently. Then we watched in astonishment as the entire front row of people in wheelchairs simply got out of their wheelchairs and began to walk! We also watched thousands of people streaming forward to give their lives to Jesus.

Every day I was wrestling inside as the call to Africa grew stronger and clearer. I remember Reinhard challenged me, "You are wrong to think that your call is to take this back to Britain. You need to understand that God's harvest fields are ripe at different times. Africa is wide open now and ripe for harvest! We need workers here!" Somehow I couldn't get my mind around the thought of giving up my company and trusting God to support us as a family with our little baby.

It was this frame of mind that allowed my old stubbornness to rise again, and I began to resist every idea of surrendering to God's plan to come to Africa more permanently. But it was in this moment when God broke into my world with the shout of "Loose this ass! The Lord has need of him!" As I have already shared in the opening pages of this book, God intervened, shook my stubborn donkey ears and miraculously rescued Rachel from a terminal coma after the accident, and healed me from my fractured pelvis and spine injury.

The remarkable thing about the accident was that my spirit was awakened and I realized something significant as that 7-ton army truck hit us. I understood in my spirit that, if the devil didn't want us in Africa, then it proved conclusively that God did! Just before we boarded the plane to fly back to England on our stretchers, courtesy of President Mugabe, God clarified the call to Rachel: "I want you to be back here in Harare, Zimbabwe, in January 1986, to be part of the prayer team and the CfaN Fire Conference."

Back in the UK, my mother nursed us back to health in her home and at the same time took meticulous care of our baby Nicola, her granddaughter. My parents were incredible in their kindness and generosity and it was a safe place to process the pain, confusion and trauma of nearly dying and losing Rachel. But it was also an extremely frustrating and confusing year too. After two months of rehabilitation in my parents' home, we were able to move back to our own house. My pelvis had healed and I was able to walk again and was anxious to get back to work, earn some money, and kick start my recruitment business. But I was torn as I also wanted to get back to Africa and out of this crucible of constraint. Rachel was still living in a wheelchair. Each day as I worked, she struggled to look after Nicola, now nine months old, from her wheelchair. Her legs were still not healing, yet every time the church prayed, some more bone tissue grew to strengthen her severely fractured bones. By June 1985, after further surgery, her legs had become strong enough for her to begin to learn to walk again. In my frustration, I decided that I did not want to wait until January next year, the time Rachel had sensed when we were leaving Harare, I wanted to go now! I reasoned we just needed to get out to Africa and start missionary life, so I arranged for a friend to take over our company and got ready to move.

Ray McCauley, pastor of one of the largest churches in South Africa, had been invited to speak in our church on spiritual gifts the following weekend. While he was preaching, he suddenly pointed at me sitting in the back row and explained to the congregation, "now let me illustrate how the word of knowledge works." Looking directly at me, he continued speaking and said, "young man, God has shown me that you are trying to run ahead of His plan. This is a time to just serve your leaders here, until it is God's time for you to move!" It was like a spiritual slap in the face which brought me straight back to earth. So I tucked myself back into the life of the church, serving them as their administrator.

The other puzzling factor was that we had contacted CfaN to ask them if we could join them and they had replied that they had no suitable position for us to fill, and, secondly, they had no base in Harare, Zimbabwe. At this time the CfaN team was based in Johannesburg, South Africa. Despite these contradictions, the call of God just kept getting stronger and stronger and, by the end of the summer holidays, we were both convinced that we just had to obey our original sense and plan to be in Harare, Zimbabwe, by January 1986.

Rachel's legs were increasingly getting stronger and she was beginning to walk, so I took a courageous step and talked to the elders of the church about our call. Earlier in the year, they had dismissed it and said that they had no peace about us going to Africa; however, as I shared what was going on inside us at this time, unanimously all the elders said, "we now all believe that you should go, and we will encourage the church to support you." The door had opened, so I called Ray McCauley in South Africa and asked him if he still felt that it was wrong for us to travel and join the CfaN team with Reinhard Bonnke. He remembered giving me this word earlier in the year but said that he felt the timing had shifted and he immediately gave us his blessing.

In the remaining weeks of 1985, we sold our house but then God told us to give away all our other savings and trust him. The church committed to fund us £300 a month and there was a groundswell of prayer support from all our friends. We booked our tickets out to Harare and decided to travel after Christmas but our main problem was that CfaN were still not based in Harare but rather in South Africa.

It seemed that God had got the details wrong and I was beginning to feel the weight of my responsibility. Here I was taking my wife and a 20-month-old baby right across the world, to a city where we had no job, no salary and no friendship base or connections. Remarkably, though, this call was so strong that we could not deny it and so we kept focused on what God had said and were still willing to go.

The night before travelling, I felt a deep sense of spiritual turmoil: "I must be crazy! What on earth am I doing?" It was about 10 o'clock in the evening South Africa time, but I felt I must call someone in the CfaN office and alert them to the fact that we were still committed to fly to Harare the next day. To my amazement, the General Manager, Peter Vandenberg, answered the call. "Gordon, how fantastic to hear from you!", he said, "we have just finished our board meeting and we have decided to close all our operations in South Africa and move our team to our new base in Harare, Zimbabwe. We would love you to join us. When can you be there?"

I calmly told him that we would be ready and reporting for duty the next day! We were the first team members to arrive in Harare and had the unusual task of welcoming the rest of the team as they arrived! What a test of God! Later, when we met Reinhard and shared the story, he said, "Wonderful. I would not have wanted you on our team, if you had not been tested! When all hell comes against you in future, you will not back down, because you will know beyond all doubt that this is the call of God." I wanted to scream but now understood the importance too – it had been the most testing year of our lives!

10

THE MALAWI MIRACLE

We arrived in Harare even before the CfaN team and as soon as they arrived we joined the prayer team with Suzette Hattingh. However, within a week, Reinhard called me into his office, "Gordon, God has spoken to me, that you are to be my Crusade Director. I want you to go up to Blantyre, Malawi, and organize our next national crusade." I was flabbergasted and said, "What on earth do I do, I've never organized any large Christian meetings, let alone a national crusade!" Reinhard smiled, yet his reply was to change the whole course of my life, "Ah, this is easy! Just go and do what the Holy Spirit tells you to do! Now go – and we will give you a car so that you can drive up there."

I had no idea where Malawi was in relation to Harare and so asked for some maps. But Reinhard explained there is only one road and instructed us, "Just drive up north to Lusaka, Zambia, and then turn right and drive about fourteen hours and you will find it!" It was well over twenty hours of driving, especially with all the border crossings and endless police road blocks along the Lusaka – Blantyre highway. Eventually we arrived, exhausted, and were welcomed by a British businessman with a church planting wife, who offered to let us use the basement flat on their property as our first home in Africa. We settled into our new family accommodation and tried to imagine what adventures lay ahead. Our little daughter, Nicola, was blissfully unaware that her bed was now a suitcase which was rapidly upgraded to a drawer!

"Just do what the Holy Spirit tells you to do!" These words rang in our spirits and, fortunately, being married to my very prophetic wife, Rachel, it was not long before God spoke to us from Exodus chapter 34 verse 10. Here God states that He was planning "to do wonders never seen before in any nation" and that He would turn the nation to Christ. As we prayed, He showed us that the keys we needed to establish were unity, persistent prayer, and working together in faith. So I called all the ministers together to discuss what God had said but soon I became aware of a strong spirit of control operating through one of the pastors. He insisted that only he should be the chairman of the committee and immediately installed himself as such! My Holy Spirit alarm began to sound loudly and, after I met with him further, I quickly decided that it would be impossible to work with him and that I should not accept him in his self-appointed role of Chairman.

I later discovered that this pastor had started his ministry well enough with a remarkable gift of healing but, after receiving unwise advice and excessive amounts of money from an overseas mission, he had become arrogant and tempted by the lifestyle money can buy. Unfortunately, when the money ran out, he began to use his power and influence to demand that his key women preached the "gospel of prostitution". Using his powers of witchcraft, he intimidated them by placing a razor blade on their stomach and then stating that this blade would lacerate their inner organs if they did not serve God by giving their bodies in sexual acts as a service to God. The razor blade did indeed disappear and through this witchcraft, and their terror of being lacerated if they disobeyed, he controlled their lives.

Furious about his loss of face, the now rejected Chairman was determined to remove us too and so he sent us a letter which he cursed through his black magic and voodoo powers. Unknowingly, we opened this letter as it arrived in the mail, and the moment we touched it we both began to vomit! A curse had alighted on us. Unsure about what you do in such circumstances in Africa, we ran downstairs to the church that was below our office and asked for their wisdom. Fortunately, the missionary pastor understood these demonic ways of Africa and suspected what had happened and carefully instructed us. We took the letter outside and burnt it, had the pastors anoint us with oil and pray, and the curse was broken. Very soon after this, we found unity and humility grew and then a prayer revival started in the churches. For weeks before the Crusade, the churches were packed at 6 o'clock each morning as Suzette mobilized them to pray for a national transformation.

Part of the curse spoken against us in this letter stated that we should be thrown out of Malawi and expelled from the nation. A few days later I was summoned to Lilongwe, the capital of Malawi, by nine leaders of the missionary movements that had been located in Malawi for at least a generation. They sat me down on a chair alone, facing them all as if at a military tribunal hearing, and then they proceeded to tear both me and CfaN apart mercilessly, saying that they would make sure that I was thrown out of the nation. They had believed rumours that we had "bought off" hundreds of pastors and asked them to work for us and that after the crusade we were going to plant our own CfaN churches using all these pastors whom we had "stolen". There was nothing true in these stories but I could not persuade them that these were all lies.

Next I received a phone call from the Inspector General of Police in Lilongwe. "You people are back again!" (I had not been told by the CfaN management that we had been thrown out of Malawi twice before, in case it would impact my faith!) "You must leave immediately and can never return: please submit your passport and it will be stamped 'Prohibited Immigrant' and then you must leave." Somehow God gave me a gift of faith and I decided to go and see one of the cabinet ministers to ask for help. This minister had a child who was unwell and he was struggling with a lack of sleep. As I prayed for him, the Holy Spirit touched him deeply. As a result he told me that he would arrange a personal meeting for me to meet with the Inspector General of Police.

I turned up in Lilongwe, with the newly appointed chairman, and was ushered in to see this powerful man. For ten minutes I simply shared with him what God had said to us, and that we believed that CfaN may well be able to answer some of the problems that were crippling his nation. Something seemed to be happening in his heart and the Holy Spirit was deeply touching him. Suddenly he got up and took all his phones off their hook and locked his door. Then he knelt by his chair and asked us to pray for him. I couldn't believe what I was seeing! He then stood up and walked over to open the door and addressed his waiting staff: "These people have a message from God for our nation! I want you to give them everything they need to succeed!"

Rachel was given the support of one of the Government ministers and was asked to organize a State Banquet so that Reinhard Bonnke could be introduced to the government! The President himself could not attend but sent his Deputy as well as the Speaker of the Parliament. Sitting together with these men and many other government ministers, Reinhard stood and shared with them what he felt God was saying to their nation of Malawi. As Reinhard closed and asked each of them to surrender their lives to Christ, the Speaker of the House immediately responded, lifting his hand into the air, together with several other Ministers. From having been almost expelled from this nation, we were suddenly witnessing a miracle at the highest levels.

The Blantyre Crusade started the following evening, on the open field outside the National Stadium. Our technical team had arrived with their huge caravan of trucks from Harare and they had set up a huge platform, sound system, lighting and toilets. The government had refused to give us permission to put up the 34,000-seater tent and also refused to let us use the 75,000-seater stadium. In faith, we set up on the field opposite the stadium. What happened next became known as the "Malawi Miracle" as, within a week, an estimated crowd of 150,000 people packed onto this field. Many travelled by bus from the other end of Malawi, all because they had heard: "Jesus is in Blantyre!"

Thousands came to Christ but, even more surprising, was the power of God that was present on the field as countless miracles of healing happened before our eyes. We witnessed a demoniac who arrived in chains, who was instantly delivered, stand on the platform, clothed and in his right mind. So many crippled people threw away their crutches and people jumped out of wheelchairs. Many blind and deaf people were healed, but the most thrilling for us was a blind man whom we had watched stumbling onto the field night after night, who asked for healing every night, finally get healed. On the final night there was a disturbance on the bus park and when we ran over, we realized people were jumping with joy as this man who had been blind since birth could now see!

We held two other crusades in Malawi, one in the capital of Lilongwe, and the other in Mzuzu in the north. Such was the historic breakthrough in Blantyre, that the government of Malawi called Reinhard to come and address the Parliament and explain what had happened in Blantyre. Once introduced, Reinhard picked up his Bible and began to explain to them how the power of the blood of Jesus can cleanse an entire nation. As he continued to speak to them, the Holy Spirit fell on the government and many of them felt deeply convicted by God.

When he had finished, the Speaker of the House announced that they were going to adjourn Parliament and that he was giving his Speaker's Chamber to Reinhard: if anyone wanted personal prayer, they were to make their way to see him in these chambers. So many came to see him and knelt in repentance and allowed Reinhard to pray for them. They estimated that over half the Government of Malawi gave their lives to the Lord! This was indeed the "Malawi Miracle": God had indeed performed wonders in this Nation that we had never witnessed in any other national crusade yet.

As we reflected after the event, we realized that as we had stepped out and simply done what the Holy Spirit told us to do, a whole nation had been turned towards Jesus. This stubborn donkey was learning to be harnessed and God was beginning to allow us to carry His glory from city to city. In trying to understand why God had moved so powerfully at this time in Blantyre, one of the team did some historical research and he discovered that Blantyre was Dr Livingstone's first missions base. In his diary Livingstone had written that they were sowing the Gospel with their own blood and tears and were just seeing a handful of souls rescued from the dark spirits of Africa. However, he said that years from then, men would come to this city of Blantyre who would reap a mighty harvest of souls!

We arrived exactly on the centenary of the founding of Livingstone's Mission. Thousands had been swept into God's kingdom, extraordinary wonders had been seen by all, and a whole nation had somehow been turned by the Spirit of God. We had simply been a link in the generational flow of an Almighty God, answering the prayers of a man who, 100 years before, had sown his life sacrificially to bring Christ's salvation to Africa. It was a humbling moment, but what an inspiration as we continued to pray bold prayers for nations to turn to God.

11

KENYA AND WORLD HORIZONS

During a time of prayer, Reinhard had a strong urge from the Lord to move the CfaN base up to Kenya. So the department of change was on the move again! This new strategy enabled CfaN to have an East Africa base in Kenya, as well as establishing a West Africa base in Nigeria. From Malawi, I moved my family up to Nairobi and initially we lived with the Wycliffe Bible Translation team who had a guest house for missionaries. Rachel was pregnant by this time and we were expecting our second child. David, our son, arrived very rapidly on January 29th 1987, in perfect time for Rachel's mother who happened to be visiting us in Nairobi at the time. Having arrived in a new city, we had made our church home in the International American AoG congregation, led by Pastor Jimmy and Mary Beggs. So, when David was born, they very kindly took us into their home and looked after Rachel, Nicola and our gorgeous new baby while we quickly adjusted once again to a new nation and life.

I was praying, fasting, and really seeking God about how we could get through all the layers of red tape so that I could see the President, gain his favour, and register CfaN as a legitimate organization in Kenya but it was like banging my head against a brick wall, as every approach I made was countered by a minister called Kiptanui. I began to feel alienated from God, who seemed a million miles away, and I was even struggling relationally at home.

As I complained to God, asking him what on earth He was doing, He shocked me with this answer, "You are carrying offence, and if you don't fly back down to Malawi and visit every one of those nine missionary leaders who wanted to get you thrown out, you will wander round and round this spiritual wilderness getting bitter and frustrated for the rest of your life!"

He then instructed me to return to Lilongwe and to ask every one of them for their forgiveness for my attitude of offence towards them. "But Father, I was the victim!", I screamed. I was the one against whom they spoke, whom they alienated and treated badly but, in that moment, I learnt a priceless lesson: God is utterly good, but often it does not feel like He is being very nice! At times, God tells us the uncomfortable truth and I knew I had no option other than to book this flight and carry out the assignment.

Back in Malawi, I made every effort to contact and visit every one of these missionaries – that is, all except one, who had been the most aggressive and vindictive! I met with the other eight leaders and apologized for the way I had been offended by them before that first Blantyre crusade. I did not excuse myself or even rehearse the past as God told me not to even mention these things. Every one of them had totally forgotten their fears and mistrust of me; in fact, they were full of excitement about the recent crusades and could only speak positively about CfaN's impact on Malawi.

Strangely, after meeting all these leaders, I still felt as if I was living inside an invisible shell. God was not going to let me off the hook until I had finished this assignment in full. I knew I had to see this last man and so I called him. I told him I was flying back to Nairobi that afternoon and asked if we could meet at the Lilongwe airport quickly, before I left. Honestly, I hoped that he wouldn't be able to make it at such late notice and I would be excused from this final encounter. But there he was, running through the airport to see me! He shook my hand so warmly and couldn't stop talking about how much their church had grown, and about how our crusade had totally changed his church.

Over coffee, I wrestled inside with my pride, but I knew what I had to say. Finally I took the plunge and started talking, "I want you to know, that I have come all this way from Kenya just to apologize to you and ask you to forgive me for my attitude towards you during the crusade. Will you forgive me?" Suddenly, heaven opened again, and my Jesus was back! The invisible shell around my heart melted, and I began to sob like a baby!

Strangely I wasn't embarrassed at all because, inside, I was overwhelmed with joy! I vowed then that I would never again become a wounded leader, I would not allow myself to take offence and become bitter. This moment sealed something in my character and, from that time on, standing for reconciliation has been one of my main core values. Later this was my motivation for setting up my ministry called Peacemakers, with the slogan – "Together, let's do the impossible!"

Once back in Kenya, I received a letter from Kiptanui asking me to leave Kenya. "The objects of your mission are undesirable to this nation, and you are now required to leave the country!" God showed me that He was in fact behind this closed door, and I was not to fight it. So, we packed all our belongings in the CfaN Land Cruiser, and drove south across the border into Arusha, Tanzania, where we found a tiny room in a Catholic guest house and fell asleep.

Christ for all Nations had already closed their base in Harare and were in the process of driving a huge convoy of giant trucks all the way across southern Africa and up to Kenya. So, under great pressure, I rapidly began renting numerous homes to accommodate the team in Arusha until we could all legally cross the border again into Kenya and establish our East Africa Base in Nairobi.

While we were waiting for these permits for Kenya, Reinhard asked me to move with my family to Manila, Philippines, and organize another crusade in the downtown area of this incredible metropolis. The week we arrived in the nation there was a Military Coup. In fact, right next to the house where we were staying were the satellite towers for the main TV station which became a hotspot for the coup. So we spent the day hiding under the dining room table with our tiny children, as helicopters were firing live rounds onto the streets all around us! We kept our heads low until all was safe. This was obviously going to be an intense spiritual battle for a precious nation!

The project took months, and I remember praying a very irreverent prayer one morning after even more delay, "Father, I've been working my butt off for weeks to get the churches together and launch this crusade. So what have you been doing all this time?" He must have smiled! Suddenly, the very next week, the local chairman, who was a Bishop, called me and said, "I want us to call a National Day of Repentance in Luneta Plaza, the largest venue in Manila."

It was one of the most moving moments I have witnessed as thousands of believers from all the churches spent eight hours together in serious heart repentance before God. Men were breaking down in tears and, over the microphone, were asking for forgiveness for their attitude towards one another. That day, God fused the body of Christ together across Manila, and the following week there was a unanimous response from all the leaders in Manila to get behind the CfaN Manila Crusade, which we called "The Gospel Explosion!"

The Manila Gospel Explosion needed several months to organize. During this planning season, an American couple called Charles and Francis Hunter visited Manila and held some healing meetings. They invited us to join them at their banquet and, although we were both exhausted, we just felt we had to go, even if it was just to represent CfaN. Sitting on the top table with the Hunters, whom we did not know, Charles leaned over to Rachel and asked her a question, "Do you have any damage in your body which is the result of a traffic accident?"

Rachel was flooded with so many emotions! She still limped badly with her right leg internally rotated about 30 degrees and about two and a half inches shorter than her left leg. This was the damage caused by the road accident in Zimbabwe back in 1984. She had watched countless miracles in every crusade, yet she still limped, so could this be her day? She scarcely dared to hope.

Rachel lifted her dress and showed Charles her scarred and twisted legs. With no emotion, Charles quietly commanded her leg to grow and straighten: Rachel felt absolutely nothing. He then told her to do something she couldn't do before. With her heart pounding in hope, she took off one of her shoes, knowing that she was usually unable to put both of her heels down on the floor together. Then she removed the second shoe and instantly both her heels touched the floor and we both burst into tears. It was finished – both Rachel's legs were perfectly straight and the right length! It was almost impossible to believe it, and yet there it was. God had totally healed her legs. Thirty years later, Rachel still enjoys running on her healed legs!

Manila was indeed a massive spiritual battle. Even though Peter Vandenberg and I had met General Ramos, a man of faith who later became President, it was not enough. We had the support of the Government, but unfortunately not of the Catholic Church. We had been advised to hold the crusade on the same ground, the Luneta Plaza, where we had just held the day of prayer and repentance but then the Catholic church held a ceremony on this same ground where they rededicated the Philippines to the Virgin Mary!

Just one week before the crusade there were accounts of strange manifestations in the sky and the newspapers and TV reported many sightings of the Virgin Mary. The Catholic Archbishop then made a public statement forbidding the Catholics to come to our meetings, which actually only made them curious and encouraged them to come and see! Every night, for five nights, Reinhard would preach powerfully, people were healed, but the response to the call to salvation was minimal. The people were contained and hardly anyone walked forward to give their lives to Jesus.

Suzette had trained over a thousand intercessors who gathered faithfully and prayed behind the platform during each service in Luneta Plaza. They were praying for the Gospel Explosion to happen. Miracles were no problem, there were extraordinary healings every night, but it was as if hell itself was blinding the minds of these Philippinos and refusing to let them walk free from the grip of their religious stronghold. Every night, Rachel drove Reinhard to and from the hotel and saw how desperately frustrated he was as still the people were not responding to the salvation message.

On the fifth night, we suddenly heard a mighty roar come from the intercessors' area behind the platform, and immediately it was as if there was an explosion across the crowd. Thousands surged forward to give their lives to Jesus, and the counsellors were overwhelmed. The crowd doubled the next night and since that moment something shifted in the spiritual atmosphere. The Manila leaders have said that they are living in a time of spiritual breakthrough.

As we prepared to leave Manila and return to Kenya, we heard that Campus Crusade for Christ (Agape) had allowed CfaN to move into Kenya under their registration permit and so the team had moved up from Arusha, Tanzania, to set up in Nairobi. Steve Mutua from World Vision had joined our team and had begun the task of preparing for the Nairobi Crusade. We arrived back in Nairobi shortly before this crusade and were offered a bungalow up the hill just above Uhuru (Freedom) Park where we were to hold these meetings.

No one expected to see what happened next: within a couple of days of starting the Nairobi crusade meetings, 200,000 people were packed across the hillside in this freedom park! Again thousands came to Christ with remarkable healings, but also, every night, people would come and return stolen goods to the platform and others would stand up and confess serious crimes. The police declared a national amnesty so that criminals could return stolen goods without fear of the law!

Towards the end of the crusade, we suddenly heard sirens blaring and a police cavalcade rolled onto the crusade ground. We knew that we had been kicked out of Kenya before, so we immediately expected the worst. To our utter amazement, President Moi stepped out of the cars, together with his entire Cabinet and requested to attend the meeting. We had no seats available for such dignitaries, so we rapidly improvised and borrowed what we needed from the hotel across the road.

Reinhard didn't change his message and clearly preached the gospel and, once again, the power of God swept across the crowd with thousands responding to Jesus, followed with a massive demonstration of healing. We were on tenterhooks, waiting to see how President Moi would respond.

The next day, Reinhard and several of us were invited to the palace for tea! Moi addressed us, "I have never seen anything like this happen in our nation. I understand you had problems in the past but I have told my people to register you immediately. I have also told all the TV and radio channels to relay every one of your meetings and broadcast them live across the whole of East Africa!"

Stories flooded in after this crusade of whole villages across Kenya, huddled around a radio, or a TV in wealthier places. Only heaven knows the eternal impact of these meetings. What we learnt, however, is this – that when the enemy comes in one direction to rob and steal, we can make him to flee in seven directions, if we push through in faith. The enemy had stopped us earlier when we were formally asked to leave Kenya, but now we were being befriended by the President himself and all of East Africa was being touched! We learnt that the greatest breakthroughs often happen after the greatest battles and opposition! It just takes spiritual eyes of faith to believe it and push through!

We loved our time in Kenya, though at times the work schedule was very intense and this meant a lot of separation from the family. Rachel stayed with the children in Nairobi and I organized two more Crusades, in Nakuru and Mombasa. Nakuru was memorable for several reasons: President Moi visited us again, and on the day of his visit a massive thunder storm threatened to cancel the meeting. However, the prayer team rebuked the storm and throughout the crusade everywhere around us was lashed with wind and rain, while we retained a pool of sunshine for a one kilometer radius for the entire event. It was also the place where a 40-year-old man who was a deaf mute from birth, was totally healed. We saw him preaching in the Nakuru market six months later!

It was also here that I befriended Pastor Mark Kariuki who had a small church of 500. After the Crusade, we watched it grow to over 10,000, and he then became the presiding Bishop over the Deliverance Churches.

The next CfaN crusade was to be in Mombasa: this was the entry point for Islam along the coast of East Africa, and now a Muslim stronghold. As I began to organize this crusade, all hell broke loose! Although the Catholics had cooperated with us in other Kenyan cities, here both the Catholics and the Muslims tried every ploy to have us closed down, remove our permits, and have us thrown out of the country.

One day, as I was praying against the strongholds of these religious spirits, God stopped me, "These spirits are not the problem here." Shocked I listened further as God then spoke to me again, "The reason the spirit realm is blocked here is because the leaders of the two largest churches in Mombasa hate each other, and the churches are powerless because of this division. Get them reconciled and you will see the breakthrough."

So I immediately invited each of these pastors, with their wives, to dinner in a nice restaurant – not telling them that I had also invited their "enemy". As they walked towards the table the men realized what was happening and they were furious! But thank God for the wives who immediately began to chat and catch up with all the family news. These people had all been great friends once when they were Bible School students together!

For twenty minutes the men sat silent and angry at opposite ends of the table, while the women continued to laugh and talk, and the Holy Spirit's conviction got stronger and stronger. Suddenly at the same moment they both leapt out of their chairs and ran around the table and sobbed in each other's arms! Total reconciliation! Both swapped pulpits and became close friends again, and one now has over 30,000 members in his church!

Within days, God stopped the attacks that were undermining the meetings when the headlines in the national newspaper read: "President Moi says, 'Leave Reinhard Bonnke alone!'" Moi gave us his meeting ground, and we had an amazing crusade. We later had another crusade there, and the local pastors told us that Mombasa was turning and slowly becoming a Christian city! It was here that

God spoke clearly to me that the key to liberating Muslims, and giving them a revelation of God's love, was simply establishing an atmosphere of unity and prayer amongst local believers. Many years later these lessons became the foundation of creating a ministry to Muslims called Mahabba (meaning love in Arabic).

12

WHEN GOD SHOWS HIS FINGERPRINTS

Kenya held a very special place in our hearts for other reasons: firstly, it was where I regained my Private Pilot's License, after having let it lapse during my time in the army and business. I used to fly early each morning, taking off over the Mombasa beaches at 6am, and then ended up flying solo over the game parks. It was such a joy to see the animals just below me, and I cannot describe the sense of overwhelming excitement being alone over the game parks with nothing but African bush and wild animals below. For those who have never flown small Cessna planes in Africa, you need to know how dangerous some of the African storms can be to a pilot.

Kenya was also where our son, David, was born, and later it was where God miraculously healed him of cerebral malaria, which is often a killer for a baby. He developed this in Mombasa whilst we were planning for the crusade and Rachel had to urgently drive him to the hospital in Nairobi. It was a terrifying moment for both of us, but even more terror was waiting for Rachel during this six hour drive.

Her car was stopped on the road by bandits, posing as police. But they took on the wrong woman because, as they tried to wrestle the keys of the car from her, Rachel would not let go, despite all their aggression!

Suddenly a tall white man was standing there, and he challenged the men with their guns, asking, "What on earth are you doing?" He took charge, and the bandit stopped fighting Rachel and meekly got into the car, though his friend was terrified and ran away. Somehow this rescuer brought order and carried such authority.

This tall white man told Rachel to drive to the police station in Nairobi and sat in the back of the car carrying David in his arms. At last David stopped screaming and fell asleep. Rachel reported everything to the police and the bandit was taken into custody. All this time, the rescuer looked after David and just held him in his arms.

When she was finished with the paperwork, Rachel took David from him and turned to thank the police for all their help. When she returned, this man had completely disappeared: she raced out to the guard post which controlled the entry and exit of personnel, "Where is the "Mzungu" (white man) I came in with?" They answered that they had never seen a white man! Still puzzled and watching, she continued on her way to the hospital to get treatment for David. The doctors examined the reports from Mombasa and then re-examined David but said that they could no longer find any trace of any malaria in his blood. He was healed! It was this experience that made us more aware that we entertain angels without even knowing it. An angel had miraculously saved Rachel, but also healed our son David from possible death.

The years flashed by, as we travelled from city to city, and nation to nation, eventually operating as the CfaN International Crusade Directors. However, the team used the more affectionate title of Reinhard's "Out of Africa" Directors. Reinhard had decided to "tithe" his crusades in Africa, and so now one crusade a year would be given away to the wider world outside of Africa. These obviously took much longer to plan so Rachel and I would travel to these nations for about nine months and live there during the planning phase.

Manila, Philippines, was the first of these crusades as I described in the last chapter. After several other African Crusades, Reinhard then asked me to travel across South-East Asia and "look for the fingerprints of God" to see which nation was ripe for this type of Gospel Crusade. I had never done this before and had no idea how God would show me where He wanted us to go. I travelled through a number of nations and cities and eventually drew a blank. How was I supposed to recognize these fingerprints of God? What were the signs?

When in doubt, call Rachel! I called my precious prophetic wife from Jakarta, "Darling, I have no idea where I should go!" Immediately she said, "Go to KL (Kuala Lumpur), Malaysia." "You must be crazy!", I said, "There is no way we could do a National Crusade there. It's an Islamic nation and last year a YWAM team were locked up just for handing out Christian literature and evangelizing on the street." "Go to Malaysia!", she repeated. I had learned not to ignore Rachel's prophetic instinct, but, honestly, I had no faith in what she had said about Kuala Lumpur, so I booked a flight to KL, arriving at lunchtime and out again on the same evening!

On arrival in KL, I asked a taxi to take me to the largest church in the capital. Prince Guteratnam was the founder and leader of one of the largest Assemblies of God churches there. I arrived at the reception of his church and asked to meet him: as I was ushered in and introduced, he looked like he'd seen a ghost! "How on earth did you get here? Hey! Come with me and look on my desk!"

On his desk, I saw that he was just signing a letter: "Dear Reinhard Bonnke, the Holy Spirit has spoken to us that NOW is the time for

Malaysia. Can you please send your representative to see me?" I was absolutely stunned! How does God do this stuff? I certainly could see the fingerprints of God now!

I informed Peter and Reinhard about this meeting and returned home to collect Rachel and the kids. Within a few weeks, we were back in KL. Pastor Prince was really confused, "Didn't you get my message not to come. All the churches are too frightened that this crusade could trigger a backlash from the Islamic government and result in the closure of churches."

Now I was confused, so I took a week away from KL and travelled to Sabah, East Malaysia, to pray. As clear as a bell, God spoke to me from the scripture in Joel chapter two: "Blow the trumpet in Malaysia and prepare for spiritual war! There are multitudes in the valley of decision, and it is vital you go ahead. Help these churches get out of their trenches of fear, or what they fear will come upon them." I had clearly heard God and knew that no matter how impossible this seemed, God was going to break through. However, this time we were on our own in raising the intercession army as Suzette, our Intercession Director, was not able to join us in Malaysia.

When I arrived back in KL, I was shocked when Rachel told me of her conversation with God. "Darling!", she said, "I had an amazing encounter with God last night and He spoke to me that we should "blow the trumpet and prepare these people for spiritual war for this city!"

Somehow I was able to convince Pastor Prince that this was a genuine call, and he gathered many pastors and leaders together to come and hear our story. That evening hundreds of leaders sat together ready to listen and, just as I was about to address them, my "little Rachel" signaled to me from the front row, and said, "Darling, God's just given me a Word."

I must admit that I just expected her to give a short word or a picture to encourage the leaders. So I innocently gave her the mic and watched in amazement as she mounted the platform and was suddenly enveloped in a mantle of God's anointing! She became the most anointed intercession leader and preacher in a moment!

She preached under that anointing for an hour without notes! "Who is this woman?", I thought. She was prowling from side to side on the platform and suddenly she drew a line across the platform with her foot and shouted out: "Devil! This far and no further! Back off!", as she rebuked the spirits holding the Malaysian people captive.

A former member of the Government said to me afterwards, "Didn't you see those angels behind her, blowing trumpets?" In that one meeting, my whole theology concerning women shifted, and I realized that I had seen Galatians 3:26 demonstrated in front of my own eyes – that in Christ, or under the anointing, there is neither male nor female. I had visibly watched the anointing fall on her and had watched my "little Rachel" become "ministry Rachel". I love the fact that, ever since that day, I have often been known as Rachel's husband! God's glory radiates from her!

There were three major impossibilities confronting us as we sought to hold this national outreach in Malaysia. Firstly, it was impossible to obtain a police permit for such an event. Secondly, it was impossible to use the national stadium for any religious meetings. Lastly, it was impossible for us to get a visitor's visa for an evangelist like Reinhard Bonnke to preach in KL. So Rachel went from church to church mobilizing an army of intercessors ready to stand and turn these impossibilities into miracles!

Then the miracles began to happen. I was befriended by a Tamil Malaysian police chief who was a believer: he used his influence to gain us favour and the police permit was granted. However, when I contacted the national stadium, I was given a firm refusal. Rachel and her intercessors prayed again: as a result, the Stadium changed their mind and said that we could use it, but the dates we had chosen were already booked for the semi-final of the South East Asian football trophy. So the intercessors prayed again, and we couldn't believe it when we received a phone call saying that the football event had been moved and we could go ahead and hold the event on our original dates! A special bonus was when the Government requested that all our advertising billboards should be in the Malay language. This gave us the privilege of inviting every Malaysian to come to the Stadium to hear the Gospel message.

Everything was going so smoothly as the teams of prayer warriors continued to pray for miracles. But a bombshell was about to go off. Just two days before the Festival of Life event, I received a message that said the event could proceed but it would need to be without Reinhard Bonnke as they had decided to refuse his entry visa.

It was as if the enemy was shouting, "Checkmate"! I was devastated but then I suddenly remembered an incident two weeks before: as Rachel was preaching in a small church in a shopping mall, a man had come up to her and said, "I have just returned to Malaysia from the United States and in the church which I attended, I picked up a CfaN magazine mentioning the plans for a Crusade in KL. It also had your photo in the magazine. I was so excited to read this news and prayed that God would enable me to meet you – and here you are! Here's my business card. Do call me if you need any help."

I called this man the very next morning and all I heard was laughter on the other end: "You won't believe this, Gordon!", he said, "but I have just been made the Under Secretary of State for Foreign Affairs with authority over all the consulates in Europe and the States. I'm going to pick up my phone now and call the Consul in Bonn,

Germany, and ask them to release a visa for Bonnke to enable him to fly here immediately." In my spirit, I almost felt God say, "Now, this is checkmate!"

The event in Merdeka Stadium was historic. It was a landmark event that shifted something spiritually in the nation. So many people, from varied backgrounds, walked into this arena to hear about Jesus, and found Him as their Saviour for the first time. What always thrills us is that in every city or nation in which we have preached, precious people always feel the atmosphere of genuine love, and realize that we are not speaking against them or their religion but just want to help them find true life. Only eternity will reveal the complete story of the fruit from the Festival of Life.

After all the follow-up meetings were completed, Rachel, the children and I packed up our Malaysian home and arrived at the airport ready to fly once again. Unfortunately, when my passport was examined, there were some issues with my documents. Rachel and the children, however, walked straight through the lines and were ready to board the flight. Concerned that I would miss this flight, leaving Rachel and the children to travel alone, I prayed, but after a few final hassles which were challenging I was finally allowed to board our flight and as we took off, we thanked God for every miracle.

From start to finish, our time in Malaysia was a miracle and a sign to me that God could overturn any impossibility to reveal Jesus. In my spirit I saw with fresh hope that whole nations would turn in the future and have powerful revelations of Jesus, their Messiah.

13

Reluctant Homecoming

Something remarkable had happened in Rachel's life as she led the intercessors in Kuala Lumpur. She had stepped into a powerful anointing of ministry and was hungry to learn more. Every day she used to get up very early, before the children awoke, and study her Bible using a correspondence course.

It was during this time that she felt God challenge her to systematically pray through all the prophetic words which we had recorded over the years concerning future moves of God in the UK. She wrote home to our church and asked for these words to be mailed to us and began praying through each one. I was so focused on praying for the breakthrough in KL that I was not really part of this process initially but soon I, too, began to seek God's plan for the next season of our lives.

As I prayed, I began to sense that God wanted us to leave CfaN, and these places of revival, and plant ourselves back into the seemingly barren spiritual landscape of the UK. His word to Rachel was, "This appointment is not for your disappointment, but for My coming appointment."

With these thoughts incubating in our spirits, a letter arrived from the elders of our home church, totally out of the blue, asking us to consider returning to the UK. They wanted us to take over as the Senior Pastors of the group of churches that made up West Herts Community Church (WHCC). WHCC was four congregations, with over 600 people, which Rachel's dad had planted. Rachel's parents were relocating to the States so this role had now become vacant. To be honest, every natural instinct within me screamed no! I was not ready to leave the incredible thrill of working on the cutting edge of missions with the CfaN team yet. A move back to the UK felt like a definite step backwards into the dark. So I eagerly accepted Peter and Reinhard's request to travel through South America and the Caribbean Islands to look for those fingerprints of God again and find the location for our next international crusade.

I travelled through Brazil, Haiti, Jamaica, and finally arrived in Buenos Aires, Argentina. It was an exhilarating trip, meeting some remarkable men and women of God. Argentina was particularly special, where I had the privilege of meeting people like Carlos Annacondia, Omar Cabrera and others who were all ready to help us with a massive Buenos Aires crusade. Revival was in the air!

We particularly connected with Omar Cabrera whom God had used to birth one of the largest church networks in Argentina. As a young man, Omar would go to a city and fast and pray until something happened. Often the demonic principality or power which controlled that city would confront him physically, challenging his spiritual authority. He would then bind the power of that demonic power, silence its authority, and then begin preaching every day until the spiritual dam burst and people began to get saved, healed and delivered. He would then establish a strong church in that city and move on to the next place.

The revival atmosphere of the late 1980s and early 1990s was in full swing in Argentina and thousands were coming to Christ through the crusade ministry of Carlos Annacondia and Omar Cabrera, but also in the churches led by Claudio Freidzon and Hector Himenez. I remember attending a meeting at Hector Himenez's church, which continued throughout the day, every day, with thousands lining up to enter the building to hear the Gospel. I also spent time with Celsio Contreras who had been one of the men God used during the Tommy Hicks revival in the 60s and 70s.

God was moving powerfully across this nation once again. However, despite the huge groundswell of excitement in the churches about the possibility of us holding a CfaN crusade, we decided to defer to a much smaller ministry which had already booked our preferred scheduled dates for their own meetings. It was a profound lesson in humility, resisting the temptation of dismissing this smaller ministry's plans, just because of our size and reputation. There would be no CfaN crusade in Argentina at this time. So I began to look for the next adventure.

I was so frustrated when I landed in Miami as I had been robbed as I departed from Buenos Aires airport. Since all my money had been taken I just had to wait until the flight to London left in three days. With this wonderful crusade opportunity in Argentina now impossible, and no money to continue my travels, this adventure had come to an abrupt end. To pass the waiting time, and pacify my frustration, I decided to walk and pray. So I walked for three days and eventually heard God ask me a question, "What has been your natural reaction to each of the calls I have given you?"

As I rehearsed each situation in my mind, suddenly the penny dropped: each time God called me into a new season, I had reacted very negatively! I rapidly asked God to forgive me for this trait and then began to wonder why God would want us back in the UK. This temptation to run, to be wild and free, was short-lived this time and I listened and yielded to His harness again.

It was so important that God had challenged my attitude, prepared my heart and that I was ready to listen to their request, as the elders of the church were at the airport, wanting a reply to their letter. After God's dealings, I was able to graciously accept their offer, subject to a short delay, as Reinhard had already asked me to organize one final crusade in Europe before I left the team. The crusade was to be held in Lisbon, Portugal, and so we were able to use this opportunity to invite members of our new WHCC Church to come across to Lisbon and experience the crusade life that was so familiar to us.

Reinhard is a man who recognizes the call of God so, as I told him about my sense that it was time to return to the UK, he listened carefully and then said, "You must obey God's call, but I want you to find someone exactly like you to take over as the International Crusade Director." It was typical of God that He put on our hearts a friend who was a sheep farmer from Salisbury! Generations of his family looked after sheep and he had no missions' experience but he had been instrumental in his rural area of bringing together churches and hungry people to pray for revival. I reasoned that, if I had come from generations of army officers, also with minimal missions' experience, this could work! This plan of a sheep farmer might appear crazy, but it was probably God!

So, John Fergusson, the sheep farmer from Salisbury, took over from me and served Reinhard globally for years, fulfilling his task with excellence. His brother, Rob, went to serve Brian Houston in Hillsong Church in Australia, and became the lead pastor of Sydney's City Campus, and a loved teacher in the Hillsong Bible School. What a great family!

Looking back on those precious years of serving Reinhard Bonnke and the Christ for all Nations team, we both feel so privileged to have been a small part of the booster-rocket which launched CfaN into the global harvest fields. As we fell away, like the booster engines disconnecting from a rocket, we were thrilled to watch CfaN continue to rise to remarkable new heights in terms of their global impact. Over the next thirty years, CfaN was to record over 75 million people responding to the calls to make Jesus Lord of their lives. It has also been such a joy to watch Reinhard seamlessly passing the burning torch to Daniel Kolenda, who now leads the CfaN team.

On our return to England, we were miraculously enabled, through the generosity of many gifts, to buy Rachel's parents' home in Kings Langley, as they moved their ministry base to San Antonio in the States. We slowly began to put down our roots again and establish ourselves as a family back in the UK. I took over the leadership of these four churches, and the King's School in Harpenden, plus many other responsibilities for missions. We were touched by the welcome we received as we adjusted to life back in England. However, the honeymoon period did not last long!

My new role included being one of the governors of the church school. As such, I was expected to put my children into the church school for their education. However, I began to find that this duty of being the church leader, and my need to be a father to my children, started to cause issues for me. The church school was situated a significant distance from our house and being out of the home from 8am until 4:30pm each day was taking its toll on our son. He was only four years old and still adjusting to a very different life back in England after being born in Kenya. Finally, we decided we needed to find a different school for David. Miraculously God provided the perfect answer. Unfortunately, this heart for our children was not understood by some and rumours began to swirl. Although we did believe that the church school was an incredible adventure and provision for many in our church community, we knew it was not the best path for our children. We took the courageous step and removed our children from the school and soon realized that God was in charge of all the details!

While I was out walking the dog one day, I met a really friendly older man, and so we began talking. Soon I discovered he was the Bursar of a local private school and he was fascinated to hear our stories from our days in Africa. One day, to my surprise, he made me an offer, "You know, we have several bursaries available for people from military and church backgrounds, and they have not been allocated yet. I would like to offer them to you!"

So both our children attended excellent private schools, with the best education, right until they went to university. One day, when feeling the heat of criticism about not having our children in the church school, I asked God to speak to me and confirm we were doing the right thing. Then at a conference, a prophetic lady identified Rachel and said that she needed to invest in her children's education because our children would be world influencers and it was important to position them in a culture where they would be trained for greatness.

I soon had an inkling of this leadership when our seven-year-old, Nicola, came running outside, clasping a toy JCB digger, telling me that I needed to pray and order a digger now. This particular weekend I was utterly frustrated as I was trying to remove the rotten roots of dead elm trees from the front of our property. It was taking hours with little success. Suddenly Nicola appeared with her digger, saying, "This is what you need to ask Jesus for, Daddy!" I was not very gracious and shooed her away back into the house.

The next morning, aching from head to toe, I was awoken by the doorbell. To my amazement, there was a JCB sitting on our drive!

"You ordered a JCB, mate?", the driver shouted as I came to the front door. "No! I am sorry, I didn't", I shouted back. "Yes, we did! Yes, we did!", squeaked little Nicola, as she ran past me to talk to the driver.

It turned out that he had got the address wrong but he loved our little Nicola so much, he promised to come back later in the day. This he did, and in no time at all he pulled out every tree root and charged us nothing! That was the impact of little Nicola and David, after seven years marinating in the faith-filled atmosphere of CfaN: they expected signs, wonders, and miracles to be happening all around them.

As parents, we often underestimate how much spiritual atmospheres shape our kids, both positively as well as negatively. We treasured the prophetic words spoken over both Nicola and David as young children. We loved watching them growing up in those revival atmospheres and it is thrilling now to watch the masterful hand of God shaping each of them for their personal destiny.

14

CHURCH AND KINGDOM – CITIES FOR CHRIST

Now began the next seven-year period of my life. It was a rapid learning curve of discovering how to lead this network of four churches. I realized that we needed to create twin tracks of leadership so that the life of the church and wider Kingdom projects could flow seamlessly side by side. So we set up the Cities for Christ team, who reported directly to us for the mission and wider aspects, while all the everyday church matters were overseen by the elders. Steve Maile and Stuart Angus, who had been trained by CfaN, became the central figures in this new Cities for Christ team. We had an excellent eldership team, who were all anointed to oversee the church family matters, but the wider missional projects were not necessarily their passion.

The first year we put up a 1000-seater tent just below St Albans Cathedral, gathering all the St Albans churches together for a crusade called "Jesus 91". It was not fair to place this financial faith responsibility on our local elders, so I guaranteed that we would personally step out in faith and believe that God would cover all the associated costs outside the church's budget. God covered all the costs, which ran to tens of thousands of pounds, and so many people came to the Lord during those days of mission, with Rachel powerfully mobilizing intercessors to break through the spiritual opposition.

Many different groups of people opposed us but, one night, the head witch of the local coven asked us to pray for her. Rachel and a friend prayed until well past midnight as she was delivered from many demonic powers. She was then able to live with someone in our team and become part of a family until she was able to plan a new life in Canada.

When we first knew her, her educational qualifications were minimal as she had missed so much education due to the trauma of her upbringing. However, when we met her eight years later in Canada, glowing with the Holy Spirit, she had just become an Assistant Professor of Genetic Engineering! Even more mind-blowing was that the doctors discovered that she had two brand new ovaries, totally free from all infection and disease, when they performed her medical check before she took her new post. What a God of grace!

All our church matters were obviously brought to our eldership and step by step God enabled us to move forward with a plan to release all four churches into autonomy. One morning, while I was praying, God showed me that the four churches were like four adolescent daughters with hormone problems! He told me that if I didn't plan their restructure, and help them develop wider relationships, they would all become religious and sterile. God showed me that we needed to eradicate our empire building mentality, humble ourselves and learn to serve the other churches in our area.

The first church to be released was our St Albans Church. God told me to give this church away and "marry" it to the Elim Church in St Albans, where I had become close friends with their pastor, Dave Campbell, during the "Jesus 91" outreach. So, on Valentine's Day, I took Dave out for coffee and told him that God wanted us to give him our St Albans Church. I was amazed when Dave replied and said, "God spoke to me last night and told me you would ask to merge our churches, but instructed me that I had to wait for you to offer to release your church to us first!"

That day we got "engaged" and, a few months later, we had a "wedding service" when both churches became one new church, forming City Church, St Albans. We were not to know that, within a few months, our original lead pastor of our St Albans church, Dave Barker, was to tragically die with cancer. But, by then, God had already secured all the sheep into a new fold.

The second reorganization involved our Watford church, which partnered with the older congregation from the Assemblies of God denomination. Although smaller in number, the members from this AOG church had fascinating stories and experiences: one elderly lady loved entertaining us with stories about Smith Wigglesworth and his meetings, while Ron Hibbert, one of their founding elders, talked of how his father was the man who caught Wigglesworth when he fell from the pulpit and died while preaching. Having caught Smith's body, Ron's father also seemed to catch Wigglesworth's healing anointing, and began to move in miracles, seeing people cured from cancer.

After this merger with the AOG church, we converted their building into our WHCC Hub Office and were located in Watford. I was also accepted as an AOG Minister and soon became their Mission's Director to the Muslim World. In 1998 I was able to hand over this Watford church to Tim and Helen Roberts, who became superb leaders and built new premises for the church in Watford called Wellspring.

The third partnership was joining our Garston Church with another small church plant and one of our elders, Roy Young, became the lead pastor, pioneering an extraordinary church planting ministry across some of the most rural parts of India.

It was not long after this that our Hemel Church joined with the Partners in Harvest movement with John and Carol Arnott from Toronto. Our Hemel elders took possession of the old British Gas HQ buildings and formed Haven House which for many years became the conference venue for most of John and Carol Arnott's UK and European conferences. Looking back on all these relational connections, I realize that only God could have steered us through such a minefield of church politics.

Cities for Christ kept active throughout all this restructuring: after "Jesus 91" in St Albans, we put up a 2000-seater tent in Hemel and had a powerful time of witnessing to the city. We still meet people who came to the Lord during that Tent Crusade and tell us their stories.

Then in 1994 we took over Watford Stadium and invited Reinhard Bonnke to preach to the whole area, having saturated the town with prayer and leaflets, with a movement we called "Love Watford", working together with Agape ministries. When the day arrived it rained, it hailed, it snowed, and the storms blew so not many people came; even some of the team stayed away because they assumed it was cancelled but we did persist. However, the several thousand who did come, looked like a drop in the ocean compared to the size of the stadium.

"Gordon!", Reinhard said wisely afterwards to encourage me, "we are fighting on a different plane here. You have no idea of the forces of darkness aligned against you. Let's see what God does in the future!" Reinhard could somehow see through into the spirit realm and he was sure that, despite the seeming failure, God had a plan and His purpose would not be thwarted.

The final restructuring was with our King's School in Harpenden. We began to partner the school with the UK YWAM base located next door. Soon YWAM began to run all the pre-school activities, to complement our primary and secondary education. The school had been birthed by the vision of our WHCC churches but it had become a little insular in its approach and it was thrilling when Clive Case came over from Ray McCauley's Rhema Church School in South Africa and agreed to take over the leadership. It has now grown to be one of the shining lights in the Christian Schools' movement.

One of the most remarkable memories of the school was when revival broke out for several months. The Holy Spirit used to fall in the school assembly and children would often receive clear prophetic words for each other, which would release deep emotional and even physical healing – often overrunning the allotted assembly time. It was a credit to all the teachers that they flowed with this move of God.

Steve Maile had been the primary evangelist amongst us on the Cities for Christ team, while Stuart Angus was a visionary leader who mobilized huge youth teams every summer into short-term mission. The first trip was to Ostrava in the north of the Czech Republic. We took bus loads with about 120 young people across to Ostrava: what a masterpiece of logistic work!

We were not expecting to step into a move of God but, as we began our outreach into Ostrava, holding street meetings in the city centre and then crusade style meetings in a large theatre in the evening, the people responded. During the ten days of mission about 700 people came to Christ! The newspaper headlines reported: "Church conquers Ostrava!" and then the radio began to tell the city what we were doing. People were not only coming to Christ but also some significant healings were happening on the street and in the theatre.

I remember one night seeing a gang of Goths in black coming to mock us at the back of the meeting in the theatre: amongst them was a young girl with a huge rat on her shoulder! When Steve Maile gave the altar call, she ran forward because she was so impacted. The gang quickly gathered round her and dragged her back to her seat.

I knew I had to talk to her, so I asked her to come outside the meeting. As I talked to her, it was as if there was a spirit blocking her from responding. Instinctively I knew it had something to do with the rat. I reached over and grabbed the rat, bound the spirit operating through it, and put it on my shoulder! Immediately, the young girl was in tears and surrendered her life to Jesus! I'm not sure that I would include this action in the any counsellor's manual, but it worked!

For the next three years, Stuart arranged these missions, in the Czech Republic, Bulgaria and Turkey. One interesting fact is that when they went back to Ostrava, the atmosphere had changed: now it was resistant and heavy and hardly anyone responded to Christ. We learnt that breakthrough is not just breaking through a wall which, once confronted, falls down and does not regrow. It is more like cutting through a spiritual membrane and then having to hold the gap open so that the scar tissue does not grow back and close the gap, making it even tougher. So, if this open heaven is not maintained through constant prayer and praise, the place where once it was easy can become tight and resistant to the Gospel.

A vivid example of this is illustrated by the seven churches in the book of Revelation, which were all in South Turkey. They all saw a measure of remarkable breakthrough but all of them finally succumbed to the demonic powers which confronted these churches. Today, these areas where the churches once thrived have become some of the most Gospel-resistant areas of Turkey.

15

FIRE FROM HEAVEN

It may sound strange after all the incredible God-stories of the previous chapter, but as the leader of this network of four churches, I was deeply frustrated. So much had happened, so many people had come to the Lord and, in Kingdom terms, we had seen some significant breakthroughs. However, when we arrived back in the UK, I had seen something in my spirit so I expected to see waves and waves of young people being swept into the Kingdom, and then to watch them in turn traveling in waves back out to the nations.

Soon after taking over the churches, we invited Ray McCauley from South Africa to preach in our Watford church. In the middle of his preaching, he suddenly stopped and said, "I believe that this city is going to have a youth revival, and it will eclipse what is happening across the nation, in terms of youth ministry." I instantly assumed that this would be one of our ministries; after all, we were the most successful church network in the area – and we were Pentecostal!

A few weeks later, a young curly-haired British-Greek came to see me: he was called Mike Pilavachi, and an Anglican! My private thoughts were, "What could possibly develop out of the Anglican Church?"

"Can you help us?", Mike started, "we've only got a bunch of twelve teenagers, but we've got a passion to start a youth movement."

God brought me back to reality with a bump. "This is it!", God said, "this is the movement that I told you about. They are not from your church, so you can't control them. All I want you to do is pray for them and be like spiritual midwives who will stand alongside and help them birth this Kingdom seed." At the time we had just opened a twenty-five bedroomed hostel in Watford which had the confusing name of God's Will. A confusing name because people would have conversations like, "I feel that God is saying it is my time to move out of God's Will", or, "I wonder if God's Will is the right place for me to recover for a while". If these conversations were heard by visitors to our church, unaware of this premises and its unusual name, people were often mystified! So Mike and his group of twelve disciples regularly met together in the big lounge area of the hostel, until they grew too big and also had to move out of God's Will!

They were a passionate group, with a couple of young teenagers called Matt Redman and Martyn Layzell who were beginning to write some quite promising songs! The group doubled in no time and then, during the first summer, they used our church building in Watford for their summer gathering. By the following summer they had hundreds join them for the first Soul Survivor Camp at Shepton Mallet Showgrounds, and from then on it mushroomed into thousands, until they were touching about 35,000 youth each summer festival! This changed the face of youth ministry across many nations, and certainly renewed the Church of England, and injected youth and life into the dwindling denominational churches.

We were privileged to be watching the birthing of one of the most precious moves of God – in the Anglican Church! It was a move which not only influenced the way we worship as a church globally, but it also infected tens of thousands of young people with a desire to see a new vibrant style of church emerge in their towns and cities.

It was during those summer camps in tents and caravans over the next few years that we connected with many of those who are now leading significant ministries today: Andy and Michelle Hawthorne, who later birthed the Message Trust, impressed us as a couple who were totally committed to the power of prayer and ready to give their lives in sacrificial evangelism. They would reshape how we reach the broken in our inner cities and transform our impoverished communities.

Prayer was at the heart of everything we did as a church and as a ministry. It seems remarkable looking back on it now, but we held 6am prayer meetings, Monday to Friday every week, and people faithfully came! I seem to remember that I attended most of them, as Rachel was needed at home with the kids who were still small. At one stage we moved the prayer meetings to the top of a building in the centre of Watford. We were hoping to rent this particular venue, which had a potential of 700 seats for our Watford church, from the local council.

We had a good working relationship with the council, police and the social services. Even though the final negotiations for the contract were taking much longer than expected, they allowed us to pray in the building every morning before we had signed the paperwork. So we prayed, we prophesied, and we stood on the roof and spoke blessing over Watford. Other times we walked and prayed through much of the centre of the town, but always calling on God to touch Watford. In many ways, I felt as if we were back preparing for a crusade and we were battling through in prayer before we saw the breakthrough in the city.

One of the mysteries of those years was that, after all this prayer, hours of negotiations and considerable expense for the planning, even with so much favour and goodwill across the town, we never occupied this building. We discovered that there was one signatory who refused to sign the contract. Unfortunately he militantly refused to allow any church of our character to have a building in the centre of Watford. This was a profound lesson for me to learn: one battle had been lost, but in Jesus we are still "condemned to victory"– if we do not give up! God had other plans and the Kingdom was far larger than the loss of a building.

It was now May 25th 1994, and my frustration levels were also growing at the lack of real Kingdom power being manifested in our own churches. Without telling our church, I had begun to travel to other places whenever I heard that God was moving there in power. This had been happening for about three months and it was then on this day, May 25th, that I heard about a new church plant being opened in Guildford by a young vibrant Australian pastor called Ashley Schmierer who had just established the base of his Christian Outreach Church (COC) movement in Brighton.

As Rachel was away teaching in Northern Ireland, I jumped into my car with a couple of friends from our church and sped down to Guildford. We arrived at the venue early and helped put out the chairs ourselves. Then the worship group began to sing but their ability was limited. However, when Ashley Schmierer stood up to speak, I was on the edge of my seat. God was here and, as I felt His power, I was desperate to have a fresh encounter with Him!

As soon as Ashley had finished speaking, I ran down to the front, but before he could even pray for me, I was thrown to the ground by what seemed to me to be a lightning bolt. I am a quiet, reserved ex-British Army Officer, not given to displays of emotion; but I began to scream at the top of my voice as wave after wave of a million volts poured through my body while lying on the floor! God kept increasing and increasing the intensity of His power, until I was pleading with Him to stop as I was afraid I would die!

I think most of the church left perplexed, leaving me alone as I writhed on the floor. I hadn't realized it, but I discovered later that I had been cursed by a witch who had cleverly manipulated her way into the home of one of our leaders. As the fire of God burned through me for almost an hour, I apparently went blue, with my hands curled up in agony from the pain, as God set me free and broke the power of this demonic attack!

Something profound was happening and a new fear of God gripped me, as this fire from heaven burnt through my whole being. About an hour later, my two friends picked me up like a sack of potatoes, and dumped me in the car as I just could not walk. As I sat there in the car, suddenly it was as if God drew back a curtain in my spirit and I saw into the spirit realm. I could see waves of the fire of God sweeping through the Muslim nations across the world and I began to roar in tongues (a mysterious, spontaneous flow of prayer in the Spirit). In that moment, I came to faith that God was going to sweep through the Muslim world with a revelation of Jesus and that millions were going to be touched by His fire.

Remarkably, that same evening, Rachel called from Northern Ireland, "Darling, the fire of God was on me tonight! I was teaching on the Holy Spirit in this Methodist church in Omagh, and whenever I touched someone, I felt as if sparks were flying out of my hands and people were thrown to the floor!" None of them had ever seen anything like this and many were filled with the power of the Spirit.

At the end of the evening an older man came forward and spoke to the church, "I was reading in Wesley's journal this morning and I believe this may explain what we have seen tonight. According to Wesley, 'when Divinity touches humanity, how can humanity expect to stand.'" "Tonight", he explained, "God has sovereignly come and touched each one of us with His fire and so we fell in His presence."

It was only weeks later that I discovered that on exactly that same night the fire of God had also fallen in the HTB church in London, when Eleanor Mumford arrived back from visiting the revival which had broken out in Toronto. As she had stood and shared her story with the staff, there were extraordinary manifestations of the Spirit happening in the room.

Obviously in the synchronized timing of God, a fresh wave of the Holy Spirit's fire hit the shores of the UK on May 25th 1994, and everyday church as we knew it was about to change dramatically over the next few years.

The following Sunday, I stood up in our church in Watford and, as I tried to explain what had happened to both Rachel and me that previous week, God just broke out in our service! Suddenly, as if a wind blew, the whole back row of the church fell off their chairs onto the floor and then people all over the building were on the floor either laughing or crying!

Over the following weeks, we just responded to this new outpouring of God's power. In every meeting, people were being touched deeply by the Spirit, many were testifying about deep emotional wounds being healed in an instant as they reached out to God with fresh hunger. This move of God flowed through all our churches and through the school, touching our children too. However, when God begins to move in ways we cannot fully understand, this often causes a human reaction of fear or aggression. So, in the midst of all this blessing, we began to see a polarization of those who wanted to flow more with this new expression of the Spirit and those who were fearful and wanted to withdraw behind more structure and control.

Within weeks, our Hemel Hempstead church had split and, not long after this, our Watford Church also encountered difficulties. It was an intensely painful time for me as a Senior Pastor to watch our sheep being challenged in this way, but there seemed to be nothing I could do to prevent the shaking, other than to remain strongly harnessed to God as He led us through this time of visitation.

I knew so many pastors across our region due to my work with the Cities for Christ crusades, and we all decided to have a few days' retreat together at the Catholic Retreat Centre to try to understand what was happening. I'll never forget the moment that we all stood in a large circle in the main hall and began to sing Amazing Grace. Immediately the presence of God began to get stronger and stronger in the room. Within a few seconds everyone was either thrown to the floor, jumping up and down with joy, laughing or crying. It was quite extraordinary!

I believe it was at that meeting that someone got up off the floor and said that God wanted to break off every debt in the room. Then, one by one, a few people shared about their personal debts, and, each time, another of the pastors in the room committed to pay off their debt! Despite all the pain of watching some churches split, a new unity of spirit descended over the churches of West Hertfordshire area. I have seldom experienced such a depth of unity, love and fellowship as I did in those days: God was with us!

16

RELEASING GOD'S HEARTCRY

When we returned in 1990, my respect and admiration for Rachel grew so much as I watched her navigate the choppy, chauvinistic waters of the UK. The apostolic network overseeing our four churches had a definite blind spot concerning women in ministry. Rachel had just been leading a prayer movement of thousands of believers in Malaysia who followed her wisdom and courage as she led the way to an extraordinary breakthrough which changed the nation. But I will never forget that, on our return, she was taken on one side by a network leader and told that women should not preach or have any leadership in the church. He recommended that she should just find her place, teach the women to honour their husbands, and how to keep their bathrooms and toilets clean!

We are not rebellious people so we took their advice and just submitted to this counsel. It was, however, just like putting a mature eagle into a tiny cage. Slowly my Rachel began to die: physically she was sick all the time, and I watched her becoming marginalized and dislocated within our own church. Then church politics began to isolate me further and I was being pulled away to be with the men more and more, losing my time of connection and intimacy with

Rachel. I often communicate through poetry and I remember writing a poem to her about feeling surrounded by a winter landscape, longing for the sign of spring. Things came to a head that Easter when my precious Rachel was sick again in hospital, and suddenly a deep primal cry erupted from her, "Gordon, I can't do this anymore! I have to do what God has made me to do: I was born to preach! I need to fly again – I need to be free!"

God heard this deep cry and, within weeks, He answered us. A friend, who led a large network of churches both in the UK and overseas, asked to come and see us. When he arrived, he explained that God had put us on his heart recently, and he had a request for Rachel. He continued his conversation by saying, "as a movement, we all believe in the principle of women in ministry but recently we realized we have never actually had any woman minister in our main summer conference. I have never heard you preach but God has highlighted your name to me again and again recently and so I have come to invite you to be the main speaker at our conference."

I remember travelling to the Brentwood Arena, still struggling with the feelings of isolation from Rachel and the confusion that this chauvinistic spirit had caused us. I felt I had lost my Rachel but, at the same time, I was being criticized by respected leaders for allowing Rachel to speak. Then Rachel walked to the platform, picked up the microphone, and began to preach. Suddenly my precious eagle spread her wings out and began to fly; my caged Rachel was instantly free! The Holy Spirit fell and everyone was sitting in tears as she ministered straight from God's heart. I sat there sobbing too as, instantly, the fog had cleared, our relationship was healed! My eagle was back and I vowed in that moment that I would never allow anyone to cage my Rachel again.

Of course, I immediately wrote to our overseers and told them that I could no longer agree with their theological constraints concerning women and that our whole church network would need to leave their movement. Not only were the churches free to function in new ways but we were both free to follow the Holy Spirit and lead together again. Rachel began to teach alongside me in the church and produce teaching materials on prayer and the prophetic gift. At last the limitations and constraints of this last season were broken and Rachel and I were harnessed together once again to pursue God's adventure.

She began to be invited to different churches to minister as they heard about the anointing she carried. In 1994 God spoke to her about forming a ministry called Heartcry. This ministry would carry three distinctives: prayer, the prophetic, and missions: it would teach people to release their cry to God in prayer; it would train people to recognize God's voice and carry His prophetic word; and, finally, it would look outwards towards those in need and show them kindness.

It was a clear vision, yet we had no idea how we should launch this ministry, but we knew it was in God's hands. Shortly after receiving this mandate, Rachel received a phone call from Northern Ireland, "We've taken our whole church through your video teaching series but we would now love you to come and do the practical final session with us and pray for our whole church."

It was my wonderful nation of Ireland that became the launchpad for Rachel's ministry and the ministry of Heartcry. For several years, she would criss-cross Northern Ireland, travelling through every denomination, stream and new church movement, until she became a household name in many of these places. With my military background, it was several years before I felt it was wise for me to join her.

The first time I accompanied Rachel as she ministered in Northern Ireland was at Hillsborough Elim Church. Now I knew Hillsborough well as it had been my first base in Northern Ireland over fifteen years previously when I had been on duty at the Maze Prison as a soldier. There was no Elim church present then but I did remember praying in a house on a hill, just outside the prison, with an older farmer, Mr. Robinson, and his sons Robert and Steve.

All these years later, I arrived at this church to find a large auditorium and, at the door, was Steve waiting to greet me! "Wow, Steve! What happened?" I was so excited to know that I was connected to the roots of this church where Rachel was now about to preach. God had moved powerfully in this area and they had birthed a summer conference called the Hillsborough Bible Week which played a big part in transforming the worship culture and attitude to the Holy Spirit in the church of Northern Ireland.

But God also had another reason for reconnecting me to this area, this church, and the Robinson family again. I knew Robert and Lorna well from my time in the army and I had even been present in their car when Robert had had a heart attack and almost died. Unfortunately, as I chatted with them and other members of the family, I realized that, although they all loved Jesus, there had been pain and misunderstanding that had pulled these brothers apart. We talked for hours, and then Robert finally said, "Let's drive down to the church and see if anyone's there who could arrange a reconciliation meeting."

I will never forget driving in the dark down the long drive from his home towards the church. Suddenly Robert pulled the car over just before the old bridge and sat in silence for what seemed like an eternity. He just sat, shaking his head, and sighing deeply. When Robert tells the story, he always says, "There is a place by the old bridge where Robert Robinson finally faced his pride and died."

After this moment, he turned, looked straight at me, and said, "Come on. Let's do it! I'm ready to humble myself and apologize." As we drove past the church, we were surprised to see the lights still on, and discovered the elders were inside even though we had no appointment – it was a God set-up.

Soon the tears were flowing as Robert humbled himself and asked them if they could possibly forgive him for his wrong attitudes which had caused such pain. I believe that only Heaven can truly record the fruit and impact of these times of reconciliation.

It is stories like this which made me realize that Rachel and I were indeed harnessed together as a mother and father to the nations, just as many had prophesied. Leaving Northern Ireland, the call to be a peacemaker had been reawakened and this love of watching people, churches and nations reconciled began to characterize so much of my ministry. Rachel continued to travel, going to place after place with her mamma heart, and soon became known as "the woman who makes grown men cry!" Wherever she ministered, people felt that she was preaching just to them. It was not long before she had grown a wonderful ministry team of women who travelled with her and ministered alongside her. This led to increasing calls for her to minister to women throughout the UK, which in turn led to the decision for the Heartcry Team to regularly book the Swanwick and High Leigh conference venues for conferences of hundreds of people. God, however, was ready to stretch her even further out of her comfort zone.

At one of her Swanwick conferences, she began to notice that men from another conference were sneaking into the back of her meetings and being deeply touched. In the break time they came and spoke to Rachel, "Why have you made this just a women's conference?", they asked, "please, you should open this up to both men and women together!" And so began the birthing of the "Shoulder to Shoulder" weekends, with hundreds of men and women signing up together for these conferences, but with the leadership still in the hands of the Heartcry Team. It was a brave move but so many men testified that it was this female-led atmosphere which created the perfect environment to minister deeply into their hearts.

My "ministry Rachel" was truly out of the box and Heartcry was becoming recognized across the nation. Rachel was often invited to work alongside national church leaders when they were wrestling with key decisions. Her prophetic gift grew and grew, along with focused words of knowledge, with countless people testifying to being healed through these prophetic words and the focused prayer of the Heartcry team. I was so thrilled that my precious eagle had finally been released from the religious trappings that people had tried to use to silence her. At last we were both experiencing a new freedom and joy as we ministered to His people. We were now ready for new exploits together!

17

DRAWN TO THE ARCTIC

Having watched the miraculous way in which Ireland had opened, we were soon to step into a new adventure up in Norway. I had fallen in love with Norway as a teenager, first visiting this nation on a school expedition aged only 15. We walked for days in the mountainous area of Lapland, after which I chose to stay longer and caught a boat down to Kristiansund and then hitch-hiked alone all the way back to the UK. Then aged 17, before I joined the Army, I returned again and trekked alone up to Narvik in the Arctic. When I had run out of money, I needed to find a job, and soon found myself working in a fish factory over in Henningsvaer in the Lofoten Islands, teaching English to the manager's son.

Now you need to know that any mention of Norway has always brought a knowing smile in our household. You see, as a young man smitten with Norway, I had my whole life mapped out and I knew it definitely included a gorgeous blond, blue-eyed, Norwegian girl with a passion for skiing! As a young army officer, my main passion was skiing, and I regularly spent four months every year on skis, leading an army ski team. God obviously took note of my self-centered obsession and smiled because I found that I actually fell in love with a dark haired, brown-eyed missionary girl from India, who hated the cold with a passion, and had no interest in skiing!

When we got married, I shared my passion for the Arctic and northern nations with Rachel; she just laughed and talked about her passion for the hot, tropical climes. As you will have noted from our story so far, Rachel's preference for the hot, sultry lands seemed to win the day. For the first ten years of mission we criss-crossed the globe, through Africa, Asia and Latin America; but God was smiling as He opened the next call of missions, and Rachel slowly began to fall in love with the Arctic!

The call came from Brian Mills on behalf of the DAWN prayer committee, "Rachel, would you be willing to go to Hamar in Norway. The Pentecostal Movement of Norway have asked us for help in birthing a fresh prayer initiative." She flew into Oslo airport and then caught the train up to Hamar. On arrival at Hedmarktoppen, in Hamar, the prayer conference committee looked puzzled, "We were expecting a Richard Hickson?" It was only later that she discovered that several other men had already been asked to do this conference but she was the only one who had responded. "Okay, we realize there has been a misunderstanding here", they concluded, "but I am sorry it is difficult for us to have a woman as our main speaker in these plenary sessions, as this is a Pentecostal leaders' conference and we prefer male speakers. Do you mind if we alter your speaking programme and you do the seminars, as we have another speaker, Pastor Lee, arriving today who is from Cho Yonghi's Church in Korea? He can take the main sessions." Rachel agreed to this change of schedule and said she was just happy to serve them as was best. The committee then went to collect Pastor Lee from the airport and discovered she was a woman too! They had been hijacked: only God could do this!

As it happened, Pastor Lee's English was not sufficient for the translator to be able to work with her, and so the programme reverted back, and Rachel spoke at all the main sessions. However, she had an ally in Pastor Lee, who held her feet while she spoke on the platform, and interceded for her throughout every message in this way. She told Rachel that she had thousands of intercessors in Korea praying for these meetings. Within minutes of Rachel beginning to preach, these leaders were in tears, and soon many of them were on the floor as a fresh spirit of prayer engulfed them.

So, as Rachel began to minister on prayer from the north to the south of Norway, these precious warriors cautiously opened their hearts to her message, and began to soften and change. This encounter opened a door for us that has kept us busy for over 20 years and we have both fallen in love with this precious nation and have travelled regularly together to every corner of this land.

It is impossible to mention by name all the places and people that entered our world at this time as they were all special. However, Hedmarktoppen Bible School in Hamar became a meeting place for us over the next years. It was here that we connected with Eivind Froen, whom I had first met in the Pensacola Revival, and who then became Rachel's translator for many years.

It was during a women's conference at Hedmarktoppen that the power of God miraculously touched Margaret, Eivind's wife. At the end of one of the sessions, Rachel was called to the back of the room and was asked to pray for Margaret: she was now unable to walk and was suffering with numerous physical ailments. As Rachel reached her hand out to pray for her, a strong sense of indignation rose up within her and all she could do was scream, "No! No! No!". As she screamed these words again and again, Margaret began to shake violently. Rachel felt embarrassed and a little confused by this violent prayer but, before she could process her reaction fully, she was ushered back into the conference and asked to close the meeting. When she had finished, she discovered that Margaret had already been taken home.

Apparently, Margaret shook non-stop for two weeks and then began to dance around the home: one by one each of her life-threatening illnesses left her body! She was totally healed, and testified in many places about her healing. Sadly, years later, in one of those mysteries which we will never understand, Margaret struggles with ill-health again today.

Tromso also became a significant place, right up in the Arctic circle, where we connected with Magritt Brustad who boldly developed a prayer project which connected both the church and the city together. Her weekly prayer meetings in the Cathedral and the Town Hall inspired hundreds across the churches of the north to pray. Many prayers were answered, and the statistics of crime and family life improved, attracting the attention of the non-Christian mayor.

At the annual thanksgiving and prayer service in the Cathedral, Magritt took a risk and invited this non-Christian mayor to come and pray with the church for his city. The whole way through the meeting, the mayor was visibly shaken and deeply challenged by the love he saw being expressed for Tromso and its leaders. Then Magritt took a brave step and handed the mayor the microphone, asking him to share his heart. She knew this moment would either be wonderful or terrible but she did it anyway!

In the event, she was astonished as the mayor spoke passionately about his new support for prayer and what he had seen change across the city and he gave numerous examples of many specific prayers being answered! As he came to close his talk, he began to shake his head, and finally said, "Tonight I have come to believe in the power of prayer and even the power of Jesus!"

The newspapers later printed an article outlining some of the miracle stories that had happened in answer to these prayers. In fact, the front page showed a photo of the Town Hall before dawn with one light burning in the main chamber: "Tromso sleeps", the article proclaimed, "but the Christians are praying for us!" How we long for this same testimony to become a reality right across our cities of Europe.

It was in Kristiansand, however, where a vital connection was forged. Having met a couple called Øyvind and Bodil Valvik at the Hedmarktoppen conference, a friendship developed, and, later, when Oyvind left his banking world and became the senior leader of Filadelfia Church, Rachel was invited to his church to preach. As she taught on prayer, this church's leadership team carefully implemented all she had taught and watched as miracles began to take place in their city.

She was then invited to speak at the Fellesmotene and became the first non-Norwegian woman to be the main speaker at this annual gathering of all the churches in the city's cathedral. I will never forget looking at the centre spread of one of the national newspapers after this event: it had a photo of Rachel with a microphone, speaking to the large Norwegian crowd in the Cathedral, and the banner headline asked the question: "Rachel Hickson: A spiritual mother for Norway?"

This report was written by a well known secular feminist editor who had met Rachel at a press conference with all the other news reporters earlier that day. Initially, she challenged Rachel in a hostile manner, until Rachel asked her why she, of all people, was questioning Rachel's right to speak as a woman. Somehow God gave Rachel a perfect key to open the door to her heart and, as a result, this editor actually attended the first evening in the cathedral and listened to Rachel speak for five minutes, before she left to write her article. She was obviously deeply moved, and returned to her office to listen to the remainder of the talk on the radio, which is why she talked of Rachel being a spiritual mother for Norway. Still today, Rachel is loved all across this nation.

It was in those early days that she prophesied, along with others, that Filadelfia Church would one day open a Jesus Centre, right in the centre of town, that would become a voice to the nation. This church continues to have a Wednesday prayer meeting every week and everyone recognizes that this is the powerhouse for everything else that flows from this church. Over the years they have reached out to the other churches in the city, connected to the business people, and found favour with the local authorities. They have been entrusted to oversee the education of a huge percentage of the city's children through their kindergartens and now influence a national network of Christian kindergartens.

They also spearheaded a work amongst the alcoholics and drug addicts and pioneered another outreach amongst the older generation in the city. They diversified further to care for the migrant families now flowing into Kristiansand too. Twenty years since we first met them, they have opened a building right at the heart of the city called Q42 which is a sign and a wonder in the Christian world. This Q42 building has a congress centre and concert hall for 1,300 people, complete with TV and radio studio; it also has 68 apartments and 8 smaller apartments for social housing. It houses an 11-room hotel, a leisure centre with sauna for seniors, and a great restaurant. Seldom have we seen the Kingdom of God so impacting a city at every level through one local church working in seamless unity together with other Christians.

I think it was God's sense of humour that Eivind Froen then persuaded Rachel and me to begin several years of ministry even further north, travelling up to the Faroe Islands in the middle of the North Atlantic near Iceland. Eivind had been part of a revival which swept through these islands years before. We were astonished that about a thousand people attended our first Easter service on this island where there are more sheep than people and the total population on all the eighteen islands is only about forty-nine thousand! The quality of the worship group and musicians blew our minds – they could have ministered easily on any international platform. Our whole family fell in love with the Faroes, and we have returned there to minister several times. Rachel was falling in love with the Arctic – but not the cold!

Perhaps the most extraordinary Arctic adventure for Rachel was when she started ministering in Canada. In 1998 in Vancouver, she prophesied over a missionary who had returned home from Pond Inlet, Baffin Island, having given up all hope of ever breaking through in the Eskimo villages of the north. But, because of Rachel's prophetic word, this missionary was willing to return for one last attempt to break through.

To set the scene, in 1928, 70 years earlier, a CMS missionary called Jack Taylor had a clear word from God about a revival fire landing in Pond Inlet and sweeping across the Arctic. But exactly the opposite seemed to have happened: the villages became gripped by drugs and alcohol and a history of tragic child abuse ensued. Jack Taylor even lost his own life after a tragic hunting accident. His family kept returning faithfully, year after year, but, eventually, even they left disillusioned. After this prophetic word stirred hope again in this missionary, he gathered people to pray, hoping against all hope that this time they would see the promised revival fire. Rachel had no idea about any of this background story but the heavenly clock was ticking, and, exactly 70 years after this word about a revival fire had first been given, the Holy Spirit fell in Pond Inlet! The event was actually captured on a tape recording. The worship group were singing at the time. However, they suddenly became aware of a steadily increasing roar of wind which began to fill the whole building with the presence of God.

Suddenly people began to shout, "Fire! Fire!", as they either fell down under the weight of this heavy presence or screamed and ran from the building. It shook the whole building and the wind sounded like a 747 jumbo jet! People across the entire area came under the strong conviction of the Holy Spirit and threw drugs, alcohol and witchcraft items out into the streets.

Within a week almost everyone in the area had made a commitment to God, and a movement started from Pond Inlet to evangelize across the Arctic and into Siberia. A year later, Rachel was given a copy of the recoding of this meeting when the fire of God fell in the village. All the letter said was, "This is your inheritance!".

What was remarkable was that, when Rachel then played this tape of the revival wind in some meetings in Dublin, immediately a lady came to Rachel and said that they knew Jack Taylor's wife and his daughter, Faith, and had their contact details in Abbotsford, Canada. Miraculously, we were speaking in Vancouver the following month and so were able to arrange to meet with them while we were in Canada. We had such an emotional time with them and, as we played the cassette of the revival wind, they were deeply moved! It was as if years of loss, pain, disillusionment and sadness just rolled away.

After the prophetic word of 1928, all the wife had known in her life was tragedy. When her husband, Jack, was tragically killed while they were in Pond Inlet, she had been pregnant at the time. She moved back to the UK with a sad heart and gave birth to her daughter, Faith, alone. Years later, Faith had travelled with her mum back to Pond Inlet just to see if there were any signs of a move of God. Sadly, it was still a demonized community, gripped by alcohol and terrible sexual abuse.

Aging, and now living alone in Vancouver, Jack Taylor's wife was now listening to the fulfilment of that prophetic word from decades ago! We couldn't help but think of Simeon in the Temple who, after waiting his entire life in expectancy, was finally lifting Jesus in his arms, "Lord, now let your servant depart in peace, because my eyes have witnessed your salvation!" It was a precious moment for us to have witnessed and we both felt overwhelmed with the precision of the planning room of Heaven which had enabled Jack's wife to finally be able to say with conviction, "God is utterly faithful and will never fail to fulfil His promises."

18

THE MUSLIM WORLD AND BACK TO JERUSALEM

After seven years of leading WHCC, and having restructured all the churches into their new season, we felt that it was time to finally release our Watford church, where we were still based, to Tim and Helen Roberts. I remember someone reminding me that Tim was only 24 years old but I knew that he was God's choice and they took to their new responsibility like a duck to water. This final step effectively signaled a new phase in my life, closing the door on my position as the Senior Leader of WHCC, and giving me the opportunity to serve in a new role on the Assemblies of God (AOG) Missions' Committee.

I worked alongside Rachel as she found her place as one of the newer prayer leaders impacting Europe and the UK. But, increasingly, God was reviving my passion for missions and the AOG invited me onto their missions' team as the Director for the Muslim World. However, it was proving an uphill battle trying to convince the everyday members of the AOG churches that the Muslim harvest fields were not across the sea but right where we lived, within our own cities. To help change these mindsets, I decided to record a video message called "Treasures in Darkness: God's Passion for Muslim people" and we sent out about fifteen hundred of these videos across the UK. It was during the making of this film that I met and connected with a young film maker who had been a radical Muslim imam, seeking to islamize Africa through satellite media. He had had a profound salvation experience when Jesus appeared to him in a vision.

Together we formed a ministry called The Bible Channel. It was really this young man's project from start to finish but it was so exciting, as a friend and trustee, to be linked to such a powerful vision. I remember him wrestling with the audaciousness of his call: he was called to disciple Muslim people in their homes, with a view to planting home churches with the people who came to know Jesus.

Many of the early programmes were in Arabic, beamed via Eutelsat across North Africa and the Middle East. We were so blessed to have the support of a TV studio in Finland and another in Belgium, which kept our production costs to a minimum. Throughout this time, we kept receiving wonderful testimonies of so many lives changed through these programmes. Very soon my friend felt drawn to produce a new series of programmes in Urdu, which was his original background, and so the focus of the ministry changed to reach Pakistan. Eventually he made Singapore his base and continued to create material to reach some of the most unreachable people in the world through satellite coverage.

In the year 2000 a new missions focus was about to be presented to us during one of our trips to Norway. Eivind Froen mentioned his wider role with China Care International and asked whether I could help a friend of his called Bro Yun (often known as the Heavenly Man) to mobilize support for the new Chinese mission movement called "Back to Jerusalem".

Apparently, China's theological perspective was that the Gospel travelled west out of Jerusalem with the apostles (apart from Thomas, who went East to India!). It then journeyed through into Europe, then

Africa, and across to the Americas, before finally reaching the Eastern seaboard of China. The Chinese saw themselves in the role of a relay race, grabbing hold of the Gospel baton from the western world and taking the Gospel all the way through the Muslim, Hindu and Buddhist nations, until it finally reached Jerusalem again. Their vision was to train and send 100,000 missionaries out from China along the old Silk Road, to penetrate these age-old strongholds. I was gripped by the potential of this Chinese revival to spill out across the Muslim world with radical fire.

Bro Yun's story was released a couple of years later under the title "The Heavenly Man", and it was a Christian best-seller for two years. By then, we had registered "Back to Jerusalem" as a charity in the UK and we had organized meetings all over the nation to alert people to God's missionary movement out of China.

It was a mission which had begun in the 1920s and then was revived in the 1940s, before lying underground for many years during the times of Communist oppression. Now it was gaining momentum again. What was thrilling was the hunger we met across the nation for a deeper level of radical sacrifice which was modelled by Bro Yun. We had over 1000 people at every meeting and some meetings were over 2000 people. The message brother Yun carried was a direct confrontation to the leisure/pleasure culture of the European Church, which had largely become sterile and ineffective. We watched people weeping and on their faces before God in every meeting. If nothing else, this was a huge provocation to Christians across Europe.

Bro Yun's life story is riveting, as he was persecuted mercilessly by the Chinese authorities because of his radical faith when he refused to submit to the government's Three-Self movement. He was sentenced to many years in prison where both his legs were shattered by the prison officers: in fact, he was called "the cripple" by all the other cell mates.

Yet he still lived a life of evangelism and miracles in the prison and, at one time, he decided that he needed to fast for a breakthrough – it was recorded to last 74 days without food and water! We've met with fellow prisoners who had been with him at that time and, when asked to verify this, they spoke for a long time together and then returned saying that they couldn't confirm the 74 days: however, they then continued, "One thing we do know, is that it was definitely more than 70 days!" Bro Yun just laughs at this, as he says it is humanly impossible for someone to survive this long without water. "They just don't get it. It had to be a sovereign miracle to sustain me this long!"

One well-remembered day, after he had recovered from this fast, God spoke to him and told him to get up and walk out of his cell! He was crippled, so this didn't make sense. I spoke to Peter Xu who was just down the corridor from Yun at that time and he said that God told him to go and tell Yun to get up and walk. Peter Xu's prison door just opened miraculously, and he went and shouted through Yun's door to get up and walk. Again, totally miraculously, Bro Yun's prison door also swung open!

It was fascinating meeting with other prisoners who knew him during this time: they all confirmed the miracles which Yun had recorded, and some actually saw him physically healed and walking right past them as they were returning to their cells. They watched him walk through every security door as if he was totally invisible to the guards. God had then arranged for a taxi to be waiting for him outside. This was truly a Book of Acts style miracle!

My life was changed just by living and working alongside Bro Yun: I have seldom met such a humble, prayerful, passionate, joyful and contagious spirit. Everywhere we went, people seemed to catch the "heavenly virus" which he carried. His daughter spent time with us at our church in Oxford and I got to know his son while doing a youth conference in Sweden together. Brother Yun's children all reflect the same passion for God. In some ways, it has been far harder for him outside of China: he has been so persecuted and misunderstood by the Western Church because of our seeming inability to believe in the miraculous.

Years later, after they had left China and relocated to Germany, they received a love for Myanmar (Burma) as a family. Burma was also so special to me as my brother and sister were born there while my father was Brigade Major in Rangoon, overseeing the final release of the Japanese prisoners after the war,

Unfortunately, Bro Yun was arrested and placed in prison on a visit to Myanmar due to the lack of the correct paper work. Each day the prisoners were required to gather for corporate Buddhist worship but, as they all bowed down, Yun would just stand up and begin to praise the Lord – very loudly! Immediately some of the back-slidden Christians sought him out and wanted to know the secret of his courage and joy. Soon he was discipling these inmates and, eventually, so many other prisoners also sought him out for prayer. He tells the story so well about how he was finally thrown out of the prison as too many of the inmates were becoming Christians!

I began to travel extensively with Bro Yun and his Finnish/Swedish translator, who called himself, Bro Ren, and sometimes with Peter Xu. However, when they requested that I travel with them to China to minister to the leaders in five of the big church movements, I knew it was time to defer to Rachel's preaching and teaching anointing.

Rachel flew out to China and was taken secretly to minister to large groups of leaders in many different places. They didn't advertise the meetings and simply trusted that the Holy Spirit would alert people to be at the right place and the right time! People certainly came and they had such an intense hunger for the Word that Rachel would often be expected to preach from dawn to sunset, in two hourly blocks of time. She told me that one day she preached the entire day from Psalm 23: I wish someone had recorded that!

What became very apparent was that there was an unstoppable grassroots move of the Spirit, which was gradually penetrating every corner of China. When Mao Zedong stepped into power on October 1st 1949, he had closed all the churches, and burnt every Bible, but he couldn't stop the outpouring of the Holy Spirit. This movement stayed invisible, growing at the grassroots for the first 30 years, and then over the next 40 years it grew from a mere 800,000 in 1949 to well over 100 million today. God has a plan for China and, as the clock draws now up to 70 years since the Mao Zedong revolution in 1949, watch out for what God will do next in China!

Over the last few years, the Chinese government has again pursued the radical house church networks and are tracking the whereabouts of church leaders and evangelists. With the Body of Christ now almost double the size of the Communist party membership, the government is desperate to control what has been a completely uncontrollable viral force in the nation. These officials are skilfully sowing doubt, fear and suspicion between the churches in every area, trying to divide and rule. But we should be excited that, behind all this scheming and control, there is a big God who has an even greater plan. I am sure that China will be used as a global missionary force in the years to come!

19

LONDON CALLING

We had both developed a passion for prayer while we served CfaN in Africa and Asia: we had seen its impact on communities and nations. Now, as we stepped back into a new season of missions after pastoring a local church, we were reminded of God's Word to us, "Remember this appointment will not be for your disappointment, but for My coming appointment."

We found ourselves being drawn into the prayer networks of the nation, often partnering with Roger and Sue Mitchell and the Building Together team. We began to meet men and women from all over Britain who were passionate about gathering church leaders and intercessors together, developing regional networks, believing together in God's power to transform our cities. London, however, always had a special pull on our hearts, ever since Rachel's father had encountered some radical Islamists in East London who had challenged him saying, "It's just a matter of time before we will have the supremacy in most of London's boroughs." Our church had carried a mandate to pray for London and this provocative encounter had stirred a cry within us that screamed, "No. Never. Not on our watch!"

In 1997 God gave Rachel a life-changing vision: she found herself watching the intense spiritual battle in the churches as they wrestled for London. In this vision, she saw friends and significant church leaders that she recognized, who were bent over, looking weary and battered. All around them, in the atmosphere, was a constant demonic assignment that she knew was the enemy seeking to harass these leaders, injure and damage their children, trying to ruin their marriage relationships, rob them of their health, and steal their finances. As she watched the ferocity of the devil against these families, in her vision she cried out to God in desperation and asked Him what she could do to protect them all.

Suddenly she was transported in her vision high above London, now looking over the city from an aircraft-like perspective, and she saw thousands of people all standing up with their hands linked forming a wall, and praying. It looked like they were a human version of the M25 motorway which forms a ring road that surrounds London. As she continued to watch, light beams began arcing across from north to south, and east to west, forming a canopy of light. From one side of London to the other, a blanket of protection was being woven as a vast canopy of prayer which was being stretched over the city, with twelve supporting pillars. Interestingly, when she saw the Millennium Dome (now the O2 Arena) being built a few years later, she said this was an exact physical representation of what she had seen in her vision: a dome stretched over the city, with twelve supporting pillars!

This vision was so vivid and precise that Rachel knew immediately that God had given her the blue-print for a new prayer strategy to protect London. So she emailed a group of friends, prophetic people and prayer leaders, and asked them to join her at Ashburnham prayer centre to implement this vision and develop a plan of action. Out of this time came a strategy that divided up London into twelve sectors. We worked with Rod and Julie Anderson at the heart of the city, Roger and Sue Mitchell in the boroughs, and we began creating prayer hubs in the towns all around the M25 motorway.

Since I was now free of my daily responsibilities in the Watford Church, I moved my office across to the new Haven House building in Hemel, which was run by our Hemel Hempstead Church. Here we set up the ministry base for the newly formed M25 Prayernet. Caroline Anderson joined Rachel and me in the office, and together we began to implement this vision to pray for London.

It was thrilling to see pastors catching the vision and joining forces for prayer and, in each of these twelve sectors, stirring their people to each commit one hour a week to pray for London. We wanted to see each sector take its place so that London was covered with 24/7 prayer. This was the early birthing of the concept of 24/7 prayer that is now so familiar to us! The prayer celebrations, held monthly in each sector over this time, were so powerful and God was indeed creating an invisible shield of prayer over our city. We prayed intentionally that we would influence the different sectors of society, which we would now call the "seven mountains" of influence (media, education, politics etc), regularly joining leaders to pray in Parliament too. We collected research and statistics so that we could pray effectively for the schools, businesses, and communities across the sectors.

God connected us with the Metropolitan police, and we partnered with the Christian Police Association so that when people gave us prophetic words with warnings about activity in London, we were able to give them to the appropriate people. One memorable time, someone from the Prayernet contacted us saying that they had received an urgent warning in prayer that a white van was going to be driven into a certain area, and they sensed in prayer that it was terrorist related. The Police took this information seriously, and they later fed back to us that the prophetic word was absolutely correct!

Over the next seven years in which we were involved in the M25 Prayernet, we felt God did protect our city from many attempted terrorist plans. When we moved our base to Oxford in 2005, Rachel handed her responsibility of leading the M25 Prayernet over to Johnathan Oloyede and the emerging Global Day of Prayer movement. When, two months after this transition, the July bombs went off on the underground in the centre of London, it was a stark reminder to us that we must continue to hold our ground in prayer and keep the prayer shield in position over the city.

Occasionally, an innocent headline can quickly mobilize people to pray. One such article was a report stating that land adjacent to St Thomas' Hospital, directly opposite the Houses of Parliament, was to be bought by a Muslim organisation. The media said that, although St Thomas' Hospital wanted this land for their own development and a research centre, they had lost the bid since this other group were willing to pay double the market value to ensure the purchase. Immediately Christians began to pray that God would give this piece of strategic land back to the hospital. It felt like a David and Goliath battle but it proved the power of prayer.

I remember people prayer-walking this area, part of the Kings College land, and claiming that this ground would be protected for the right use. On the day of the planning and purchase decision, the national newspapers printed artistic drawings, showing the proposed designs for the new alternative buildings which were to be called the Islamic Cultural Centre of Europe. What joy there was that afternoon when it was reported that, due to a covenant clause found in the title deeds, this ground had to be given to the hospital for first refusal. Praise God for Florence Nightingale who had unwittingly staked this ground and protected it for its correct use just over 100 years previously! The land was sold for a much lower fee to a Medical Research Foundation in partnership with the St Thomas' hospital and, today, the Prideaux

Building stands on this land! The prayers of ordinary people had shifted the authorities and the Islamist organization, insulted by this refusal of their offer, stated that they would no longer work in London and moved to another nation.

It was in the late 1990s that we began to become aware of the influence of the African prayer movements growing in Britain. All nights of prayer on Friday evenings, led by the African churches, were becoming a common feature in our cities, and suddenly we realized that we had spiritual allies in the nation. Britain had sacrificially exported the Gospel to so many nations over the decades, and now our sons and daughters were returning to stand with us and fight for the spiritual legacy of the UK.

The Holy Ghost Festivals, led by the Redeemed Christian Church of God (RCCG), were just beginning, with around 10,000 people praying all night: today it is over 45,000 people! Pastor Agu asked Rachel and me to lead prayer at these events in those early all-night meetings with Bishop Adeboye. It was like being back on crusade with Reinhard! We were beginning to feel that God was with us, fighting for London.

I remember being called from Nigeria by Emmanuel Kure, asking me to speak to his prayer gathering in Kafanchan. I already had two other appointments during this time, so apologized and said that I could not join him. To my amazement, I then received a ticket for the flight to Abuja in the post with a short note, "Cancel your other appointments: I have set up a meeting with the Nigerian President in Abuja and then I need you at our prayer conference." What authority!

I immediately did cancel my other appointments and arranged to travel to Nigeria. In Abuja, the President was occupied but I met with his wife who had initiated 24-hour prayer for her husband and the government. General Obasanjo had earlier become a believer in prison and, once he became President, he re-dedicated the nation to God.

While in Abuja, Kure took me to see the Senate President and I was deeply moved at lunchtime when every Christian, whether Senator or cleaner, came together into the main conference hall and cried out in prayer. Soon after this, I was driven up to the Kafanchan conference and could not restrain the tears as I walked into the meeting place where 10,000 people were crying out to God for London and the UK!

I was overwhelmed with a sense of gratitude that God was mobilizing the prayer warriors of the nations which we had impacted with the Gospel in the former generation. We were not alone: Africa was returning to fight for its "mother England".

We were also deeply moved by the influx of prayer warriors and leaders from Latin America, who also arrived in the late 1990s to partner with us in prayer. It was a time when many leaders in our area had been challenged to pray and fast for 40 days on behalf of the nation. Many pastors were looking decidedly skinny!

One of the prayer leaders who joined us was Victor Lorenzo from Argentina. For years he had prayed to break the masonic influence of London over Argentina. In fact, one day while in prayer, still in Argentina, he saw himself lost in London in a vision. In his vision he watched as he came up out of an underground station and saw a man in a raincoat and asked where he was. "Oh, you're just down the road from the main Masonic Temple", came the reply.

As the vision continued, he watched himself decide to visit this masonic temple and, as he arrived, he told the old man at the reception that he had come all the way from Argentina and would love to be allowed to put on the Grand Master's regalia and sit on the main masonic throne. At that precise moment, as he was in full regalia and on the throne, the receptionist had to take a phone call. Alone for those few precious minutes, Victor declared from the throne that every masonic vow of secrecy would be broken and exposed. No sooner had this prayer ended, than the vision lifted and he was back in his room in Argentina.

Several years later, Victor came over to London for the first time to minister in our prayer conference. On his day off, he decided to do some sightseeing but unfortunately got lost. Suddenly he found himself coming out of the underground and recognized that he was living out his vision but this time in reality! However, when he knocked on the door of the main Masonic Temple, the old man greeted him saying, "Welcome back. You're the man from Argentina! Would you like the same tour?" How on earth was that possible? Victor had obviously been "translated" physically during his earlier vision!

Literally the day after this experience, when he sat on the masonic throne and broke the masonic vows of secrecy, the British Government passed a law insisting that every public servant had to declare if they were Masons. The vow of secrecy was broken! With God, the Spirit knows no boundaries or distance: we are not alone!

20

GOD'S PASSION FOR RECONCILIATION

Fueled by my own personal passion for reconciliation, I soon became involved with the England Reconciliation Coalition – a rather grand sounding name for a group led by Roger Mitchell and Brian Mills. The vision of this group was to build bridges of reconciliation and repentance with nations where our British history and actions had left wounds in their past. The group had already focused on Australia, Africa, and India.

Since the next nation in the spotlight was to be Ireland, and due to my own history, I immediately felt I needed to be involved in this journey. I will never forget praying on Vinegar Hill above Enniscorthy, Wexford, Ireland where the English soldiers killed hundreds of the United Irishmen in their attempt to hold control over Ireland. Lord Edward Fitzgerald had been one of the leaders of the United Irishmen. I knew that our family was directly linked to him, as he had married into the Fitzgerald family, and that my great-grandfather, Edward Fitzgerald Hickson, had been named after him. So I was able to stand as a direct representative in this time of repentance and prayer; to me this was extremely personal.

So together, my son, David, who was now seven years old, and I caught the flight to Ireland ready to stand and pray on behalf of our family and this nation. We immediately continued to see the fingerprints of God on this time as our host, who collected us from the airport, asked if he could stop to visit his mother in a residential care home in Dun Laoghaire. As we approached the care home, 40 years rolled away as I stood looking at my grandmother's expansive old home of Altadore, which I had visited as a child, and which was now the place where my host's mother lived! I knew that this was going to be a destiny moment for my son and me.

Two hundred years after the tragic events which had divided Ireland, my son and I stood in a circle on top of Vinegar Hill, with people from every side of the past and present conflicts, and broke bread, pouring out the wine over the blood-stained soil. We cried out to God and asked him to cleanse the stain of our English sin against Ireland and restore the nation back to peace.

At this moment we were unaware of what was happening politically in Northern Ireland that day, but the next morning the Peace Accord was ratified and signed in Belfast! It was results like this which encouraged us to keep standing and repenting for the national sins of the past, so that we could watch the timeless power of the blood of Jesus changing history and restoring nations.

Canada was another nation where we unsuspectingly found ourselves repenting for the sins of the past. Rachel and I had been invited to speak on prayer at a regional leaders' gathering in Medicine Hat, Alberta, Canada. As we arrived, we realized that these leaders were weary and many churches were struggling to achieve a breakthrough in prayer, especially for healing. Evangelism was proving ineffective, and it often seemed that Heaven was shut up. So Rachel and I prayed and asked God to give us some keys to unlock this resistance, and

160

we were shocked to hear His answer. He told us that we, the British, were responsible for the closed heaven in Medicine Hat due to past injustice!

It had been British soldiers and pioneers who had come into Medicine Hat and, while seizing this fertile land, they had slaughtered hundreds of first nation people, even killing them by distributing blankets that carried small pox. It was very clear that God was asking us to stand in the gap and clear this spiritual blockage from the past. We discovered that a Chief from the North Peigan tribe was already connected to this group and was a committed Christian. So we asked him if he could help us with this injustice of the past. He suggested that we meet at the Saami Teepee, the largest teepee in the world and a well-known feature in the city.

When everyone was gathered, we spoke briefly to them about the past history we had discovered and asked them if they could forgive our nation for our treachery and betrayal against their people and their land. I will never forget how they instantly sank to their knees and wailed: it may have been centuries ago but it was still a raw wound in their tribal consciousness.

Then the Saami chief, the custodian of this native land, explained that when the British had taken their lands, his people had cursed the fields, rivers and territory, declaring that nothing would grow, and relationships amongst the white men would struggle with misunderstanding and division: the tribe still rehearsed this curse today. However, moved by what he saw that day, he stood and, in his native tongue, accepted our repentance, chose to forgive us, and then broke the historic curse of his tribe. We had no idea that the fundamental reason for the closed spiritual atmosphere and the divisive spirit in the area was because of this curse, provoked by the slaughter of their precious people.

That evening we held a large gathering of local Canadian Christians with the First Nation believers. God spoke to Rachel that we needed to do three things: Firstly, we should give them the most precious thing we owned, as we had robbed them of their most precious land. Immediately God spoke to me and said that I should give them my wedding ring! (My current replacement wedding ring was bought in Medicine Hat.) Secondly, we should find a Union Jack flag and lay it before them and ask them to walk across it as a sign that now we wanted our nation to serve them, not dominate them. Thirdly, we should find some roses, a symbol of love and our national flower, and hand them out to the First Nation people as a sign of restored intimacy.

The evening arrived, and the place was packed, with the First Nation peoples, our guests of honour, at the front. We shared what God had spoken to us and, as I walked towards the chief representing the tribes of the First Nations people, and placed my wedding ring on his finger, we both sobbed! That day I became a blood brother to Chief Manfred North Peigan. We then entered a time of worship and asked them to process over our British flag, as a sign of humbling our nation of England. Towards the end of the evening we spoke about reconciliation and the restoration of intimacy between the British and the First Nation people.

However, the third part of our act of repentance had proven difficult to execute. Although we had looked for roses in the town during the afternoon, we could only find a handful at a local gas station. But as we walked down to begin to present these roses to this packed hall, I heard a loud banging on the rear door of the church. It was rather persistent so, while Rachel started to present the roses we had, I went to investigate. Outside the church was an Interflora truck!

"Hi. It's the end of the weekend and we have hundreds of roses left in our warehouse. We heard you had a big gathering here tonight:

could we possibly give these roses so that you can hand them out to everyone here?" We were overwhelmed with joy that evening, knowing that God was showing His fingerprints again, and sealing this time of reconciliation with His miraculous gift of hundreds of roses.

The next day, at the Sunday gathering, a church leader who had had issues with one of the local churches attended. He came and knelt at the front and asked for forgiveness from the church he had split from. Someone then prophetically said that God wanted to restore marriages, which had been another area to which this curse of relational misunderstanding and division had applied. That morning couples walked forward weeping and allowed forgiveness and reconciliation to flow. Come on God! The final miracle was that these churches decided they would keep working together, even though it had been tough. During a fresh initiative between the youth pastors, the atmosphere began to change, and young people suddenly started coming to Jesus!

This time in Medicine Hat utterly convinced me about the power of identificational repentance so I continued to be part of a whole series of prayer initiatives where I stood and repented on behalf of our history. We may not always understand what we are doing at these times, but one thing became very clear: we just had to do what the Holy Spirit told us to do, and these acts of obedience released God's power!

The next adventure was to be in Germany, which was special to me as my grandmother was a German from Hamburg. Burning with a conviction that prayer walking in our communities was shifting atmospheres, I found myself volunteering to be part of a team that would pray and walk from London to Berlin. We would be carrying a large cross and walking as an act of reconciliation focused on the atrocities of the Second World War.

I joined the team in Braunschweig and walked for a week all the way through Eastern Germany to Berlin. Each evening we had arranged to meet local Christians when we stopped, so that we could publicly ask for forgiveness for the destruction caused by the British bombing raids towards the end of the Second World War. On our team was an old British bomber pilot who was now in his 80s and I will never forget the weeping that would erupt each time he stood and asked for forgiveness. It may have been over fifty years ago, but the emotions were still raw and the memories painful as they remembered the carnage and death.

I had patrolled this border as a soldier in the 1970s, and now it was a thrill to carry the ultimate weapon of the Cross over this old border. It was during this walk that God germinated a dormant part of my family roots, as I became deeply aware of my own German ancestry. One day I found myself crying out to God in German as we walked, "Father, please forgive my nation for all our atrocities." – I was suddenly aware that I was praying this as a German not as an Englishman!

One of the historical strongholds which had blighted the German church for years was the Berlin Declaration of 1909, which deeply divided the Evangelical and Pentecostal streams from each other. It was this rift in the body of Christ which, many believed, gave spiritual permission for the division and split of the nation into East and West Germany.

As we walked across the border, we cried out to God that this old wound of hostility against the demonstration of the Holy Spirit stemming from 1909 would be healed and the Church would come together. At that time, we were told that it was impossible for this Berlin Declaration to be revoked. We arrived exhausted in Berlin one week later to discover that we had actually arrived on the exact day of the March for Jesus in Berlin! Then we were further astonished when the organizers asked whether our prayer team from the UK would lead this march.

The route of the march was through the age-old Brandenburg Gate, which was known as the symbol of the divided Germany. As we walked through this gate, our small team of prayer warriors picked up the cross and aimed it like a weapon, declaring its power would break the wicked spirits of division that had overshadowed German history.

There were 70,000 German people following behind us, but we charged like an elite fighting force through the Brandenburg Gate, praying at the top of our lungs that this spirit of division would yield. We felt something happen! The whole crowd followed after us through this gate and gathered in a large plaza where a platform had been constructed. We all watched the organizers gather on the platform and saw that they were having a heated discussion.

Eventually the chairman of the March came to the microphone and apologized, "We are so sorry for the delay, but we believe that God has just spoken to us. We feel that it is appropriate that we should all ask God for forgiveness for the years of division caused by the Berlin Declaration which has outlawed the Holy Spirit from Germany. Let us all kneel in God's presence today and welcome the Holy Spirit to return to our land of a united Germany."

That memory still sends chills down my spine! As we all knelt and prayed, on this windless, blue-sky summer day, suddenly a strong wind blew across the whole crowd. It was electrifying! It was a new day for my nation of Germany: God, the Holy Spirit, had returned!

Since that moment, I have had a burning passion to be involved with anything that connects our motherland of Britain back together with the fatherland of Germany in Europe. The enemy has kept us fighting against each other through two World Wars, but God has a Kingdom purpose for these two nations to be harnessed together in these latter days. As our nation disconnects from the institution of the European Union through Brexit, I believe that God's plan is to then reconnect us in a new spiritual alliance with our European partners which will have extraordinary Kingdom significance.

21

THE GLOBAL PRAYER AND PROPHETIC MOVEMENT

We can never underestimate the power of prayer and God's relentless generational blessing through families. From the moment I met Alan Vincent, Rachel's father, in the little Bedmond Chapel in 1976, long before Rachel and I got married, he became my spiritual father, and my whole spiritual life was shaped through his teaching. He had pioneered across India in the 1960s and early 1970s: and his fervent prayer in Bombay had triggered a revival which started in April 1972.

In a similar way to the manifestations experienced by Omar Cabrera in Argentina, Alan found himself being confronted by a demonic principality. An indignation rose up in him and he wrestled with this demonic presence in the night until it gave up and "disappeared" through the iron bars guarding the bedroom window! After times of prayer, fasting and worship, the spiritual atmosphere in the area began to shift and suddenly revival broke out in their district of Bombay. It led to hundreds of people coming to the Lord and several significant church movements were birthed from this time.

Rachel's parents were also the catalysts of the Catholic charismatic revival which swept through the communities in Bombay and influenced India. Rachel's brother, David, was unexpectedly born in Bombay at the Holy Family Hospital although the original plan had been to go to a mission hospital in the hills. However, this surprise opened a door of opportunity as Rachel's mother began to share with the medical nuns about the Holy Spirit. During a pre-natal appointment, Rachel's mum had already discovered that the leading nursing sister was spiritually hungry and had heard about the Catholic Charismatic influences touching the American church. On the day of the birth they had plenty of time to talk and the conversation continued.

After David's birth, Alan agreed to go to the sister's communal home just before Pentecost and pray for them all to be baptized in the Spirit. Twelve sisters gathered that night and they were all baptized in the Holy Spirit. From that encounter, Alan began to hold a weekly meeting in a local Catholic school; hundreds came, including some priests. Father Rufus was one of the priests who was most impacted, and he carried this fire throughout Catholic India. They estimated that thousands came to the Lord at this time.

Probably the most unexpected harnessing for adventure was when Rachel's dad met John Babu, a young pastor from Armoor near Hyderabad. He had been a Hindu policeman but, unbeknown to John, his mother had visited a Christian pastor and asked for prayer when she had discovered she could not conceive. When John was born, his mother returned to see this pastor and she had dedicated him to Jesus before returning to her Hindu practices.

Years later, when John was in the Hindu temple crying out to his gods for an answer to his liver disease and drunkenness, he heard an audible voice that instructed him to go outside and listen to Jesus. Outside the conversation continued as God then told him to leave the temple as He had work for him to do. John then saw Rachel's dad in a vision and God told John to start learning English so that when he met this man, he would be able to communicate with him. It was to be 3 years before John finally met Alan.

John was so thrilled to finally meet the man from his vision and he excitedly invited Alan to come down to his church in Armoor and preach on the Kingdom. The meetings were powerful, but John was horrified when forty out of the hundred believers left the Church because they were not prepared to lay their lives down for this type of Kingdom message!

Those who stayed, however, were filled with the Holy Spirit and a move of God started which swept through the state of Andra Pradesh. Once they had established their base in the city of Hyderabad, many thousands were saved, countless miracles were recorded, and there were three testimonies of the dead being raised! All this from obeying a vision!

It was then fascinating that Reinhard should contact us, the year after leaving CfaN, and ask us if we could help him organize a major crusade in India; and it just happened to be in this city of Hyderabad! I was able to take time away from my daily responsibilities in the Watford Church, as they were willing to release me due to the family history that already existed. I managed to quickly draw all the churches together in Hyderabad and bring a sense of purpose and cooperation for this crusade, while Rachel mobilized an army of intercessors to pray for a breakthrough in the city.

For weeks we battled to obtain a permit for the only suitable venue for the crusade. Unfortunately, this area was the massive ex-colonial Parade Grounds in the middle of the city, which were tightly controlled by the Ministry of Defence. Finally, I took a faith risk and advertised across the whole city that we were using the very small field next to the venue that I wanted, in the hope that God would move in the corridors of power and release the main Parade Grounds to us before Reinhard arrived. What a thrill it was when I received a personal telex message from the Minister of Defence in Delhi, giving us the authority to move our platform, sound and lighting onto the Parade Grounds! The telex arrived on the very day we were setting up the platform!

What a remarkable crusade with over 300,000 Hindus, Muslims and Christians, spreading out as far as the eye could see, with thousands responding to the call for salvation. I also felt such pride as I watched my Rachel preaching to thousands of believers in the CfaN Fire Conference, which was held during the day in a huge venue. Following the success of this crusade, Rachel was able to return to both Bangalore and Madurai in later years to assist CfaN in mobilizing intercessors for other crusade events.

Rachel's parents had moved across to San Antonio, in the States. Her dad was travelling extensively and teaching the leaders the principles of Kingdom church, with a passion to see prayer and worship centres bringing local transformation. "Harp and Bowl" prayer tends to focus on bringing our intimacy and petitions before the throne of God. However, in these "Tabernacle of David" expressions of prayer, it was a much more militant style of prayer which expressed a strong, authoritative prayer, ready to speak into the heavenly realms.

One evening, while at a conference in Corpus Christi, Texas, they received news that the local weather centre had released a warning that Hurricane Lily was expected to make land fall the next day. People were being encouraged to evacuate and prepare for the devastation. When the leaders heard this report, they decided they needed to rebuke this storm and pray. So people gathered together and began to worship and declare the might and authority of God over the weather. At 9.15pm, Rachel's dad felt it was the time to directly command this storm to lose its power and so everyone turned towards the direction of the hurricane and commanded it to stop and die – and then they went home, wondering what God would do.

As they read the meteorological website the following day, they saw, to their amazement, that questions were being asked as to why, at 9.15pm the previous evening, such a destructive hurricane had suddenly lost its power and turned into a whimper! As a church, we are often so unaware of the power we carry and can release in these moments of national crisis.

Armed with this family legacy of prayer breakthroughs, and inspired and empowered by our own experiences of prayer with Reinhard in the CfaN crusades, Rachel and I began to connect with the global prayer movement. Prayer and prophecy are never far from each other, and very soon Rachel was also being drawn into the global prophetic movement. We remember vividly one particular day, when Sharon Stone asked us to stand up in a meeting, "God asks you a question", she said, "what ford is it? Find the ford and you will find the place where you will open up deep wells of revival." Everyone laughed as they all knew us and the "ford" we were connected to, as we were the senior pastors of Watford Community Church. But Sharon had no idea that at this time we were considering a move to Oxford, another "ford", and so this word became part of our story of transition in the years to come.

Our connection with Brian Mills and Jane Holloway opened doors for Rachel and me to travel all over the country and to many other nations. This heralded a time of mobilizing a prayer movement which would become a catalyst for city transformation. It was during this time that George Otis released his Transformation videos, which gave hope to the prayer warriors wherever the films were seen. Rachel was able to share the story of what had taken place in Pond Inlet amongst the Eskimos with George and he was able to include this story about the sound of the wind on his next video which encouraged many.

As mentioned, we were already criss-crossing Norway with a message of unity and prayer, but then the doors to Europe opened too as this continent is so inter-connected. It was Rachel in particular who began to travel through Sweden and Denmark, Ireland, Spain, France, Italy, Belgium, Holland, Austria, Germany, Switzerland, Poland, Hungary, the Czech Republic, and through the Balkans. I travelled with her whenever possible but, for much of this time, she travelled and ministered alone, while I stayed in Watford and pastored the church. It was a hard time for her, but she knew she had to obey the call and yield to this God adventure.

On one of these occasions, when she thought she would be travelling alone, God had a special surprise for her. She had been invited to Poland to minister as a prophetic voice to their national prayer movement. When they invited her, they told her that she would share the ministry with an older apostolic father who had been a friend to the movement for many years. On arrival, she discovered that this older man was in fact her dad and so the family legacy was modelled over this whole weekend. Since Rachel's married name was no longer "Vincent", they had no idea that Rachel Hickson was in fact Alan Vincent's daughter!

The impact of the global prayer movement was very strong in these years. Mike Bickle was influencing the world with his model of 24/7 prayer in Kansas City at IHOP, while Pete Greig birthed the ministry "24-7 Prayer" in the UK in 1999.

During the summer of 2000, Mike Pilavachi of Soul Survivor and Andy Hawthorne of the Message Trust partnered together to gather thousands of young people in Manchester on mission. Rachel and I had facilitated the prayer support in a back room at the Soul Survivor camps for years but now, in this merger, Mike and Andy gave us a massive prayer tent at the centre of the campsite. 24-7 Prayer, Fusion ministry and our own prayer movement, partnered together to "infect" this new youth generation with a love for prayer, and it was such a joy to see young people passionately praying for their friends and cities day and night.

Surprisingly, it was the Salvation Army who first embraced this culture of round the clock prayer and, over the next decade, we watched the growing culture of youth prayer, particularly using a 24/7 prayer room, spreading through the churches and denominations in the UK. Modern monastic communities also began to spring up and a whole movement of houses of prayer spread across the UK and further afield, all from the unsuspecting Welsh hillside of Ffald-y-Brenin.

One of my most precious memories at Ffald-y-Brenin was sitting under the cross on the hillside, during a rain storm. The day we visited Ffald-y-Brenin it was pouring with rain but, because I had heard so many stories of people who had a profound encounters with God while visiting the cross on the hillside, I was determined that the weather would not prevent me from going to the Cross. As I arrived, very wet and cold due to the lashing rain, I hesitated but then felt God asking me, "Won't you give me just one hour of your time here?" "Father, you've got to be joking!", I shouted, knowing that I would be utterly soaked if I even stayed 5 minutes. But, drawn to this space, I found that I did sit there for an hour, with my back leaning on the Cross, with the stormy winds and rain beating horizontally into my face. I was totally soaked by the time I returned to join Rachel, who wondered where on earth I had been in such a torrential storm!

That one hour was one of my most intimate moments alone with God, with the Holy Spirit pouring through me: I laughed, I cried, and prayer poured out of me in a way that reminded me of my Korean encounter with God when I was immersed in the Spirit of prayer on Prayer Mountain.

We had both been deeply challenged by the culture of prayer in Africa and Asia. It had been Prayer Mountain in Korea which had ignited my initial passion for prayer, then Africa which had inspired us both in bold authoritative prayer; but what I have loved watching and being part of in the UK has been the amazing united, cross-church, cross-denominational, city-wide prayer movements which have multiplied across most of our major cities and towns.

As I have reviewed this journey of prayer in the nations, I have realized once again that I was born to pray, just as Rachel was born to preach. But I have to admit that I sense the Holy Spirit wooing me again to join Him on another history making, adventure in prayer. Revival is bursting with stories which just begin with a man or a woman in prayer which triggers a "suddenly" of God. I want to stand in my latter years, gripped with an unshakeable determination to provoke a divine "suddenly" of history once again because of my persistent fervent prayer!

22

Time To Cross The Pond

Even though Rachel now had parents living in the States, and we were ministering across the UK and Europe, no opportunities had yet opened for us to minister across the pond, in America. But God was about to change all this and supernaturally open up a door into the States, making America one of Rachel's favourite places of ministry.

Rachel was spiritually tired and decided she needed to take a few days away on retreat to rest and pray. One of the couples with whom we had become close during this time were Ken and Lois Gott, who were stewarding a powerful move of God in their church in Sunderland. So Rachel travelled to Sunderland for a time of refreshment and input, explaining to Ken and Lois that she wanted to come and refuel in their meetings and not minister this time. There was such a sense of God's presence and, as usual, this atmosphere began to revitalize Rachel's spirit. This was a safe place of revelation and incredible worship. After one of the morning meetings, Ken approached Rachel and asked her to pray prophetically for just one pastor that he felt needed a word from God. Rachel hesitated as she had promised God that she was there for Him alone and that she would not minister but receive. However, Ken continued and said, "As I was praying this morning, I felt God say you were the one to ask and I will only ask you to pray this one time over these days as I respect you". So, during the morning coffee break, Rachel prayed with this pastor in the auditorium and he was deeply impacted. As Rachel ministered to this pastor, she was aware that there was another man watching her intently as she prayed and prophesied. As soon as she had finished praying, this observant man leant over the chairs and said, "I would like you to come with me please. I have someone that I need you to pray for too."

Rachel apologized that she was not able to do this for him as there was a protocol at the conference that only people with the appropriate badges who were part of the prayer ministry team were supposed to pray for others and so, she suggested, perhaps he could ask them. However, he looked unconvinced, "I heard the accuracy of the prophetic word you gave during the break as I know that man. What do I have to do to persuade you to pray for my pastors?", he asked. "Well", Rachel offered, "if you ask Pastor Ken Gott for his permission, he will come and find me or maybe ask the speaker for the next conference session. If he gives me permission that he is happy for me to pray, then perhaps we can go ahead." "Well, I am the next conference speaker, my name is Frank Damazio!"

No more excuses! So Rachel turned and continued to pray for Pastor Frank's assistant and had a very significant word of prophecy for him. "Do you by any chance know a man called Joseph Garlington?", Pastor Frank asked, "If you do, I believe you must be the "Rachel" he told me to look out for in England." "Yes, I do", Rachel responded, as dear Joseph Garlington was a treasured friend of our family. To others, Joseph Garlington is an amazing pastor, preacher and worship leader who had led the worship in the Million Man Promise Keepers' March in Washington.

Pastor Frank continued, "I am having a conference in Portland called the North-West Intercessors' Conference and I would like you to come as one of our speakers." It was now God's time for Rachel to cross the pond, and so a door opened for Rachel, which has continued to welcome her over many years.

That annual conference grew to over 3000 people. Invitations to minister came thick and fast from all over the States and Canada as a result of the connections made at this conference, and it wasn't long before she was widely known as "the woman who makes grown men cry." These years at the Portland Conference drew together a variety of different speakers and ministries and so Rachel was privileged to have time to connect with many international, world renowned, leaders. It also helped expand Rachel's understanding and worldview of the prophetic prayer mantle as she had the honour of speaking with Cindy and Mike Jacobs, Chuck Pierce, Dutch and Ceci Sheets, Lou and Therese Engle, Wes and Stacey Campbell, and so many others.

Also thrilling for us were the connections that were built with strong churches who carried a similar heart, where Rachel spent many years ministering – churches like the City Church, Seattle, with Wendell and Gini Smith. Seattle became a special city in Rachel's life, as it became the place where friends like Glenda Renes and Russ and Julie Zylstra and Marlene and Bill Brubaker lived too. Glenda stepped up to run Heartcry USA, and the Zylstras and other significant friends stepped in to create a place of welcome and sacrificially supported Rachel's ministry.

It is now over twenty years, and Rachel has been crossing the Atlantic with regular frequency. At one point, we both wondered if God would reposition us to be based in the States for a period of time as so much ministry was developing over there as well as in Canada. We even had a clear prophetic word from someone we highly respect but the practical details have never unfolded. However, if we hear the call, we are ready for this adventure if it comes!

One of the unexpected blessings to come from these times of ministry in so many churches was the constant stream of testimonies of lives changed, people healed, and babies born. It seemed as if one of Rachel's hidden gifts was praying with people who are clinically barren and later hearing that they had had a child – well over a hundred people have testified about a miracle child after Rachel prayed for them!

My favourite testimony came from a New York ladies' conference. Throughout this conference, Rachel kept noticing a tall, blond lady, and every time she felt God say, "Tell her, God is going to give her two zebras!" Rachel ignored this nudging and thought it did not make sense but these "God nudges" would just not go away and continued all day. Finally, Rachel stood up to close the conference and immediately felt God say, "before you close, I want you to pray for all those who are unable to conceive and want a child." Immediately two girls got up and ran out of the meeting, only to return a few moments later with this tall, blond lady in tow! As Rachel stepped towards her to pray, she whispered in her ear, "God says that He is going to give you two zebras. Does that mean anything?" The lady instantly fell on the floor, sobbing! Suddenly, out of the shadows, a tall, handsome, black Afro-American came and stood over the blond lady. "What on earth did you just say to my wife?", he asked. Rachel quietly whispered God's message to him, at which he began to sob too!

"You have no idea what this means to us", he said, "my wife has been longing to have a baby for years and we have nearly given up. But in our personal love language of our black-white marriage, we have always had this joke and said, 'Let's make love and make zebras!' This word has to be a word from God, as nobody else knows!" Nine months later, Rachel was in tears when she received an email from this couple. It was headlined: "Twin Zebras arrive in New York". What a God!

Reams of books could be written from the testimonies which the team received from all the ministry and conferences in the States and Canada. Rachel was invited to minister into so many different networks, streams, denominations (even the Southern Baptists!), and church movements, and it was exciting to catch a flavour of what God was doing.

Rachel's parents settled in San Antonio, Texas, in 1990. They became American citizens, even buying their burial plot to remind the family they were not going back to the UK. They are now based in Max Lucado's church, after ministering apostolically for many years with a network of churches and ministries, with Outpouring Ministries. Rachel's brother, Duncan, and his family also relocated to San Antonio, and became American citizens too. America was now permanently part of our lives and hearts forever!

Rachel then formed Heartcry for Change USA, getting her 501(c)(3) non-profit registration in Washington state and confirming her sense of call to America. Once registered, God challenged Rachel to take time to pray for Washington DC and to invest and leave a legacy in this capital city too. She had already been praying for London with the M25 strategy for many years but now it was time to serve another capital as well. Rachel's connection was formed through many visits to Washington DC with Ken Wilde and his National Prayer Center. After those early years, she intentionally began to put Washington in her diary, and take regular times of prayer just to walk and bless the city. God then opened doors for her to connect with senators and congressmen and women on Capitol Hill. She learnt to love America and carried a sense of God's plans for the nation; so much so, that she committed herself to be fully involved in praying during every election, even President Trump's, after which she was invited to attend Trump's Inauguration Ball.

I remember Rachel taking a week to pray all around Washington before the last Presidential election: as she prayer walked, God showed her His plans for Trump to win the election. I was shocked when she came home just before the election and announced that God had shown her that Trump would definitely win. With my rational mind, that certainly made no sense, but then God reminded me that His ways were not always our ways. It was totally unexpected when she had heard this from God, but now she was so sure. I was in awe of her gift when the election results came out and her confident prediction was confirmed. Few had expected this!

In a similar way, Rachel has done exactly the same with Brexit. I had been a clear "Leave" advocate, and Rachel had been for "Remain". That was until God spoke to her and asked her why she hadn't asked Him what His plans were! He told her to go across to Belgium and spend three days in the European Parliament buildings in Brussels just before the vote, spending time with some of the Christian MEPs and then asking God what He wanted, and which way the vote would go. It wasn't long before she knew without a doubt what God wanted. Again, she returned home so sure, and announced that the nation would vote for Brexit!

One of the joys of ministering across the States and Canada in so many settings was that many leaders became close friends, and many places began to feel like our second home. I only joined Rachel on a few of her tours but had the thrill of hearing the stories when she came home. We both came to love Vancouver Island, and we loved the West Coast, whether in Canada or the States. She would often travel to the East coast without me, as well as countless other cities through central USA and Canada. One of her favourite networks was the network linked to Bethel Church in Redding, California, and she found herself being drawn into several churches connected with this movement. She also preached alongside a number of their team in a few conferences.

Over the last couple of years, we have both been invited to join with many other global ministries, gathered together by Mike and Cindy Jacobs in Dallas, for the Global Prophetic Summit. It is such a stimulating network of prophetic people from so many nations. It is so inspiring, as well as challenging, to be together with so many other men and women who understand what God is saying to nations.

In November 2017, one of the most moving moments was hearing from a Zimbabwean pastor who had been a catalyst in mobilizing prayer for us in 1984 in Harare, when we were run over by the 7-ton truck and Rachel almost died. As we prayed in Dallas, God spoke prophetically that Mugabe would be removed from power that day! There was an incredulous reaction at first, but then the whole gathering began to make a sovereign decree over Zimbabwe that Mugabe's time had come and that he would be removed from his position of power and control. Later that afternoon, people's phones began to pick up the BBC breaking news: Mugabe had been placed under house arrest and finally, a few days later, he was removed from power, and a new day was beginning in Zimbabwe. We all knew that the coming days, even years, would be turbulent but God was about to fulfil His prophetic destiny in that nation! One day Zimbabwe will again be the "Bread Basket of Africa."

23

Called As A Shepherd To Oxford

Most people would know about the Oxford-Cambridge rivalry! As a Cambridge graduate, I never imagined that God would one day call us to Oxford – but sometimes we have to "stoop to conquer"! It was on New Year's Day 2004 when God woke us up and showed us that the cloud had moved, and now we needed to move with it. It was seven years since we had laid down the leadership of our WHCC churches, but now God was indicating that we should close down our involvement in the London Prayernet, as well as closing the Heartcry office and get ready to move. Strangely, He laid three cities on our hearts and then was silent: Peterborough, London, Oxford.

Immediately we thought that we should explore moving to Peterborough to work alongside our friends, Dave and Karen Smith, in their faith venture with their new church building. Rachel had been used prophetically in the whole story of how they came to build this magnificent Kingsgate Church building. We looked at forty-eight houses but still felt no peace to make an offer and, until the summer, we had no plans other than moving to Peterborough.

It was at the summer Grapevine Bible week that God woke me up and told me to stop all these plans to move to Peterborough. He just said that our relationship with Dave and Karen was very important for the future but we were not to move and live there. In spite of this, we knew Peterborough would be important to us in time. Today it is, as it has become the church home for David, our son, and his family.

I then began to explore with Gary Clarke whether we should move to London and be part of all that God was doing there with Hillsong. But with our daughter, Nicola, newly married to Tim Douglass, who was now on staff with Gary and involved in so much of the leadership, we knew we should give them space to flourish on their own. Family needed to stay family; I was wise enough to realize that one day London Hillsong would also be important to us.

We were coming to the end of the year and had not solved the riddle of our future, though we still had not explored Oxford. On Sunday November 14th (I will never forget this day when God hijacked us), there was an Open Day at St Anne's College, Oxford, and our son, David, was very keen to explore this college. We drove up to Oxford and looked around the college and he met quite a few people doing Maths there. However, he didn't like St Anne's, so we made plans to leave. I then remembered that I had once visited a significant student church called St Aldate's in Oxford with Rachel's dad. It was at the time when Michael Green had been the Rector, and Alan and Michael had held an open debate about the importance of full immersion baptism versus christening: Alan was advocating full immersion baptism, while Michael spoke for the Anglican viewpoint.

We discovered that we weren't too late for the service, so we rushed over to the church and snuck in the back of St Aldate's. I was recognized immediately by the new Rector, Charlie Cleverly, as Rachel had worked for several years with his wife, Anita, when they pastored in Paris. David and I were invited to sit on the front row with

Anita. Something happened during the service and the presence of God came, and I noticed Anita sitting tearfully beside me. "God's just spoken to me", she said, "I believe He wants you to be the new Parish Vicar here in St Aldate's." I just laughed! "Anita, I'm an Assemblies of God pastor: there's no way that I could ever become an Anglican minister!"

I didn't mention that I had grown up in the Anglican world but had slammed the door on the Anglican Church at the age of 15 and had vowed never again to be part of it after my school days. After the service, I went back to their house and Charlie casually said that Anita often heard from God, "We spent all of this year looking for the right Parish Vicar but the Church Council could not find the right candidate, so we are advertising nationally tomorrow." He handed me the advert and, as I read it, I laughed, "That is exactly me", I said, "but I would never be able to become an Anglican Vicar!"

As I shared all this on the phone with my prophetic Rachel, who was preaching over in the States, I was unnerved by her response, "Gordon, I believe this is God!". So I agreed with Charlie to send him our CVs and quickly drafted one that did not disguise my non-Anglican credentials. To my amazement we were invited together, along with many other candidates, for a day of interviews with the whole church council. As we began to share about ourselves to the council, the Holy Spirit came so strongly that one of the church wardens passed a message to the others in the group, saying that they needn't look any further – I was obviously the perfect match for the job. I whispered to Rachel that I was not interested unless the whole council came to a unanimous decision that we were God's choice. As we drove home to Watford, I had a phone call in the car informing me that their decision was unanimous: I was their choice and God's choice. I cannot describe the panic I felt, but I still had one last hurdle to conquer.

I still could not believe that the Bishop of Oxford was going to allow me, a definite Pentecostal, to become a Parish Vicar in one of the flagships of the Anglican world. I did not think he would be sympathetic to my position as he was not an evangelical and certainly not a charismatic; but the Church just told me to go and talk to him anyway. I emailed my very non-Anglican CV to the Bishop and was surprised to be called immediately for a meeting the next day.

As I walked into the Bishop's office, he greeted me like a long-lost friend! "I've been longing to meet you: you and I have so much in common!" I was astonished as we were light-years apart in theology. "Here, look at your CV: you went to Wellington College, so did I. I was a 'fag' (junior helper) to David Watson when he was a prefect, before he became a great charismatic preacher – I chose another path. You then went on to Sandhurst Military Academy and then Cambridge University– so did I."

We talked for about 45 minutes about the past – nothing about theology – and then he surprised me, "You know, as a Bishop I can ordain someone on the spot, without you having to spend three years at the Anglican theological college. I want you to take this role at St Aldate's. You don't need to do the three years' training: I will just ordain you next summer." I knew I'd been hijacked: only God could have done that!

It was Spring 2005 and so began one of the most rewarding phases of my life. As we walked the streets of Oxford, I was often in tears knowing that we were walking in the very footsteps of the great revivalists: George Whitfield gave his life to the Lord in my church building after the fire of God fell on him in Pembroke College; Charles Wesley had walked these same streets and I was later ordained on exactly the spot where he was ordained in Oxford Cathedral.

I felt God speaking to me that he had called me out of my working environment of global mission strategies to learn how to love and encourage "the one", the individual. He was commissioning me to help ordinary people achieve their big dreams. One of the references Charlie received about me, which was sent by one of the most respected UK bishops, simply said, "This man is not a Pastor – he is a mission man." However, over the next five years, God worked so deeply in my character and opened my spiritual eyes to enable me to see and love people, and I truly became a pastor.

It wasn't long before God reminded us of the prophetic question: "What ford?" God now spoke to us and said, "This is the 'ford' that I spoke about – Oxford – and this is the place where you will see Me opening up the wellsprings of revival."

I won't share much here about those years as Parish Vicar at St Aldate's, other than the fact that I became part of what we called the "Dream Team". I have seldom worked and learnt so much from such a wonderful team. One of my most precious possessions is the book I was given by the church on leaving, after almost six years, with hundreds of words of deep thanks and gratitude from so many of the members. I had become a shepherd, and my heart had been changed to reflect His Father's heart. Every person, and every dream, mattered to God, and I cared so much for them!

The relationships between the Oxford churches were fairly broken, with so much division, little friendship and minimal prayer for the city. Similar to me, Charlie Cleverley also carried a passion for prayer and unity. So with my missions planning background, he asked me to try to organize a united gathering of the churches so that we could all stand together and pray for Oxford.

Charlie and I gathered a great team together from across the churches and we birthed a movement called "Love Oxford". God had shown us that we needed to address the deep wound of Oxford, which happened exactly 450 years earlier on 21st March 1556, when Bishops Cranmer, Latimer and Ridley were burned at the stake by the Catholics on Broad Street. Since that time, a spirit of division had plagued the churches. I therefore spent weeks visiting all the pastors and then spoke to the Catholic bishop in Oxford and, together, we carefully crafted a prayer of confession and repentance which everyone could agree with.

Heaven must have been on tiptoe as several thousand Christians gathered, standing right on top of the place where the martyrs were burned at the stake 450 years before. We had fifty churches together, including the Catholic bishop's representative. All the pastors and leaders stood, shoulder to shoulder, on the platform and, together with the whole crowd, we asked God to forgive us for the centuries of pain and division between the churches, and we pledged to stand shoulder to shoulder under the banner of the Cross and to proclaim Christ to the nations.

Something shifted in the spirit realm over Oxford that day and since that time, the churches have co-operated together at a different level of trust and friendship. Years later, having left this role as Parish Vicar, Rachel and I became part of the newly planted Hillsong Church in Oxford which Gary Clarke planted out of London. I feel once again that we are amongst a generation who are willing to pay the price in sacrificial prayer and action which will re-open the deep wells of revival that are ready to burst in Oxford. We are ready to be history-makers in this city once again!

What about Peterborough? Well, Peterborough soon became a family home too, as our son, David, and his wife, Jenny, and our grandkids, Annabelle and Jeremy, made Kingsgate Community Church their spiritual home. We often see our friends, Dave and Karen Smith, as we attend their church services, and Rachel is a frequent visiting preacher

– still with her prophetic edge, though very much seen as part of the family now too. The church has blossomed to several thousand people now, with church plants out into Cambridge, Leicester, and London.

24

FOR MILLIONS OF MUSLIMS
TO KNOW HIM

When we first arrived in Oxford, I really wondered as to why God had called us to close everything down in Watford and move to Oxford. For Rachel, it soon became evident that it was a great launch place for her ministry Heartcry for Change. She found that the Oxford environment inspired her to write: she has now written eight books, two training manuals, and has others in the planning phase.

The St Aldate's curate (Assistant Vicar) called Helen Azer, who kept me on the straight and narrow when I first joined the church, later joined Rachel as her Ministry Associate. She is now a world-class prophetic teacher like Rachel and has recently taken over as Director of Heartcry for Change UK. Oxford has a gift of being a springboard to nations.

As I prayed about my role in this season, however, all I heard God say was two things, "Feed my sheep not the giraffes" and "Pray for the Muslim World". I had been intimidated with the whole intellectual and theological scene of Oxford, wondering if I would be able to connect adequately. So the first time I preached, I confessed that I came from "the other place" (Cambridge), and said that I planned to feed their spirits with practical biblical truths that I had tried and tested of how

God works. I slowly began to feed the sheep and, together with the amazing team, we were thrilled as the church attendance grew to about 1500 each Sunday.

Rachel and I were asked to teach a Summer Bible School for an evening each week during the summer holidays and very soon we had over 400 people attending. People were hungry for God and, after every service, people were at the front asking for prayer ministry. The presence of God was so strong, and then I realized that people had also been worshipping on this very site for over 1000 years! We were treading in the footsteps of spiritual heroes.

I had understood how to answer the instruction of "feed my sheep" but how should I pray for the Muslim world? I had obviously grown up amongst Muslims as I spent every summer for several years from 1958-60 in Aden (South Yemen) where my Dad was facilitating the movement of British troops during the first Kuwait Crisis. Then, as a businessman birthing Construction Services International, all my work was in Saudi Arabia, Iraq and the Gulf, providing project management teams for the massive construction projects across those oil-rich Muslim nations. Then, working as Reinhard Bonnke's Crusade Director, I found myself being sent into totally Islamic cities to organize mass evangelistic campaigns.

On returning to Watford, I found that my church building was right across the road from the mosque. However, there was a ghetto mentality in the churches and none of us had any contact with Muslims. So I prayed and wrote a reconciliation statement, similar to the one I had used on our reconciliation walks across Germany. A few of us met with the local Muslim council and I asked permission to talk to the whole mosque. After reading this reconciliation statement, asking for forgiveness from the Muslim community for the fact that we had alienated them for years, their hearts opened wide to us.

They asked us if we could help them teach their wives English, even if some of it was from the Bible, as many just stayed at home and were isolated. They asked us for help with looking after their children in the school holidays as they loved what they saw of our children's holiday clubs. Then, amazingly, they asked if we could open up a place of prayer where Christians could pray for their sick, for healing in Jesus' name! Tragically, when I presented all these opportunities to the local churches, not one of them was willing to be involved!

After 9/11 happened, with the tragic deaths of thousands in the twin towers in New York, the entire Muslim community in Watford were traumatized and in fear of a vengeful backlash from the town's people. I immediately contacted all the church leaders and told them that this was a unique opportunity to demonstrate the reality of Christian love to the whole Muslim community.

I ordered hundreds of flowers and asked the Church leaders to please help me distribute them to the Muslims as they came out of the mosque after Friday Prayers. I was expecting everyone to be there to help but not one pastor or leader turned up as they were so fearful! Together with a handful of intercessors, we pressed flowers into every hand as they came out, "We understand your fear, but don't be afraid! We are the true believers in Isa Al-Masih (Jesus the Messiah) – we are the people of the Book, and we will be your closest friends through this time."

Many of the men were in tears as we presented them with the flowers. I vividly remember one young Muslim man who jumped into my arms and gave me such a big hug, "I don't know where you're from", he said, "but I'm going to follow you!" I never realized that one simple act of Christian love could leave such an impact. Conversely, I became very aware that the greatest barrier to Muslims coming to Christ was our fear as Christians! Just as we had found in Kuala Lumpur, the churches were paralyzed by fear which prevented them from reaching out towards these precious Muslim people.

Back in Oxford, as I was remembering all of this, I heard that Tim Green, the son of the former Rector and evangelist Michael Green, was returning to Oxford from Pakistan, after eighteen years of working amongst Muslim people. Tim and I became close friends and we agreed that we would combine my passion for prayer with his brilliance for training believers, and we would gather people from across all the churches at 7am every Tuesday in St Aldate's to pray for Muslims.

Our slogan became: "Face the facts – don't fuel the fear!" It was becoming so obvious that fear was the greatest hindrance to Muslims being reached. The second obstacle was that church leaders tended to feel that they needed specialist training in Muslim missions before they could reach out into these communities.

So we decided we must reach out. This Muslim outreach would be called Mahabba Oxford (Mahabba meaning "love" in Arabic) and would seek to equip ordinary Christians, trained by the mission specialists, to love all Muslims. Over the next two years, a strong committed core of friends bonded together, and Tim and Rachel Green began to systematically train many Christians through a course called "Friendship First", written by Steve Bell, which was then filmed and formed our first Mahabba training course.

Remarkably, even then, it took two years of persistent prayer before precious Muslim people began regularly to come to the Lord. Quite soon after we started, we were joined by a man who had been a radical imam and who had come to the Lord in an encounter similar to Paul on the Damascus Road. God shouted at him in his mosque and instructed him to come out and serve Him! He wandered around the streets dazed, and eventually plucked up courage to walk into a church and ask them how to be saved. His family tried to kill him and he still has the scars from the fired bullets but he managed to escape to the UK where he became part of our prayer team.

God had shown me many years before, as I organized crusades in Muslim cities, that the two keys of persistent prayer and unified relationships were essential for creating the right atmosphere to unveil Jesus to Muslim people. So many God-inspired initiatives were birthed as a result of this simple one hour of united prayer on Tuesday mornings in St Aldate's, and of course during the coffee time afterwards!

People began to prayer walk the Islamic neighbourhoods and then give each household a "Jesus Film" DVD, with an offer to return and talk with the family once they had watched it. Others set up literature tables outside the mosque and in the High Street, giving away Bibles and tracts in many Islamic languages. Some courageous Christians moved home and lived in the Islamic areas of the city so that they could pray and befriend their Muslim neighbours, leading them to Jesus. So many other God-inspired initiatives came out of this time of united prayer.

What was happening in Oxford caught the eye of the Evangelical Alliance and Global Connections, a network of mission organizations. They asked us to consider developing Mahabba networks to reach out to the Muslims in other areas and cities of the UK. So, in 2011, I left my role at St Aldate's to pioneer the Mahabba Network nationally.

Only God could have known that as an Anglican vicar, and from Oxford, I was perceived by other church leaders as a more trustworthy messenger. Although the message was no different from what I had carried as an AOG pastor from Watford, the label of an Anglican minister from Oxford carried more respect and was a winner! Hence Mahabba spread fast, not only around the UK, but also in many other nations who revere Oxford.

In 2012 we launched Mahabba nationally and there are now over sixty cities with Mahabba networks. Over these years, we have also seen it spreading out to France, Belgium, Norway, Austria and Denmark, and then across to Singapore, Korea and Australia. I've also shared the vision in Canada, South Africa, and Switzerland, and we are currently working with the Syrian migrants in Germany.

Miraculously, God provided me with a salary for three years from someone I met for breakfast at a conference in Budapest. The truth is that I ignored this offer initially because I wanted to raise my funds in a different way. It took me four months to humble my British pride and accept that God had chosen the One Mission Society, in the States, to be the midwife to birth Mahabba globally.

I finally flew out to Indianapolis to meet them and was shocked when they explained that they were a Kingdom Mission and didn't need their name on anything: they were investing into a vital new Kingdom mission. I can honestly say, that without their strategic financial support, Mahabba would never have been brought to birth. I explained all this to my prayer group in Oxford and asked them to pray with me for the funds needed to now develop Mahabba. I had a salary, but we needed the funds to rent office space, hire staff and meet expenses.

One of this group simply placed £5 on the table: "Lord, if this is you, then multiply this seed!" In the next meeting that I went to that day, I was given £50. That evening, I was given £500 by someone else. The following morning, I was sent a cheque for £5000 from someone I had not seen in ten years. I was enjoying this adventure of faith! So I opened an office in Oxford and was then sent a huge donation of £50,000 from the States! Since that date we have received more than £500,000 in donations to develop Mahabba globally.

What is so thrilling, is that millions of Muslims are coming to know

Jesus globally through dreams and visions and encounters with God. Mahabba is doing its little part in getting the church and ordinary people to be prepared globally for this final harvest.

Let me close this chapter by saying that when I had that encounter with God during the revival in Cymbran, Wales, in 2013, I wrestling with God because He was asking me to believe Him for 30 million Muslims! This experience lasted over an hour and God wouldn't let up: I was eventually so exhausted, that I finally gave in and shouted out, "Okay Lord, 30 Million Muslims!" As I rose to my feet, I knew that I had come to faith, and I cannot explain this, but God clearly deposited this seed of hope in my heart and so every day I allow this promise to germinate in my spirit. Like Elijah, I believe that I can hear the abundance of rain falling in the nations: this rain will be Muslims finding Jesus in their millions.

25

CALLED TO THE MARGINS TO REACH THE BROKEN

Although I know God has a passion to reach each individual and will always leave the ninety-nine to look for the one, there is one story of Rachel's which so emphasized this truth to me and changed my outlook on life. Rachel had been invited to preach at a conference in the Midlands on the subject of spiritual warfare. As she was preparing, God told her to change her emphasis and speak about spiritual warfare from the point of view of marriage.

On her arrival, Rachel gave the organizers the new set of notes and explained that she would teach on marriage and relationships in the context of spiritual warfare. As she spoke about the battle for our marriages due to adultery, pornography, and other sexual temptations, the Holy Spirit moved so powerfully and, as lunch time approached, Rachel knew she should stop and offer to pray with people. As an illustration to help in the response, Rachel drew an imaginary line across the front of the church: she asked if there was anyone who needed to step over this line and begin to take back all that the devil had stolen from their marriages and relationships. A vast percentage of the people came forward, with many weeping and prostrate on the floor. As most of the ministry team were already busy praying, Rachel just walked around praying and asking God whom she should pray for.

As Rachel watched, God showed her a man at the very front sobbing: "Can I pray with you?", she asked. "I shouldn't be here", he said, "I live three hours away and haven't been to church for several years. I woke up so early this morning, desperately unhappy, as I cheated on my wife years ago, which ended in divorce and I lost everything. This morning I just wanted to savour something of the joy we used to have in the past, and I drove all the way here, as it is the town where my wife came from, and we used to come here for weekends to visit the family. When I arrived here, it started raining and so I took refuge in this church, but then, as you began to speak, I was gripped by what you began to say. Can God forgive me? Is there any hope for me?"

Rachel prayed with him for God's peace and forgiveness, and then walked to the back of the room where she noticed a lady on her face weeping. "Can I help you? What is the pain you are carrying?", Rachel asked. The lady looked up and said, "I shouldn't be here; I live about three hours away. I was coming to meet my mother today and take her out for the day. But, when I got to her home, she had forgotten and already gone out. As I was walking around the centre of town, I saw this church and saw your name advertised. You were one of the last people to prophesy over me, but it was many years ago. I was fascinated to meet you again. My husband cheated on me several years ago, and we are now divorced. But, as you began to preach about the spiritual battle for marriages, I suddenly began to realize that the devil had had a strategy against us; but I also realized that I had a part in driving my husband away. Do you think there is any possible way we could ever be reconciled?"

Suddenly Rachel realized she was in the middle of a God set-up! "Will you trust me?", said Rachel, as she took this woman by the hand and led her all the way to the front of the church. "Do you see anyone you recognize on the floor right now?" "Oh, my goodness, that is him!", the lady cried, and Rachel left these two broken people together, weeping in each other's arms. God had woken two broken people up in different homes, made Rachel change her message, and had compelled this couple to make their way to a town three hours north. He had organized the weather to rain and drawn them into this church and then He began His miracle of restoration. However, that wasn't the end of the story.

About a year later, Rachel was in New York when a girl working with the Bill Wilson teams came up to speak with her. "I don't know why, but God's told me to tell you a story. I live here in New York with an English girl. A few years ago, her parents were divorced, but she had a vivid dream recently that both her parents were going to be reconciled and she would return home to have Christmas with them, all sitting together around the Christmas table. After this dream, we both agreed to fast and pray for twenty-one days to see what God would do but, throughout these days, the situation just seemed to get worse. On the twenty-first day we just said, 'Okay God: it's over to you now!'" Well, God did work on that twenty-first day and began to reconcile her parents. Of course, this was the same couple Rachel had prayed with in the north of England and now she was able to hear the back story of a daughter's prayer for her divorced parents! By the next Christmas, the full reconciliation had taken place and the whole family sat in tears together as they gathered in wonder around the Christmas table. This is the God I love!

What a remarkable revelation of the heart of God! So often divorced people feel like such failures, so broken and hurt; they often feel like second-class citizens and wear a cloak of shame. Far from rejecting them, Father God is longing for people to get busy in prayer, and grab hold of these lives, so that He can restore everything that the enemy has stolen.

It is this awareness that motivates both Rachel and me to spend time ministering to broken people because it is at these times, more than any other, that we witness the power of God to set people utterly free. These transformed lives, rescued from the pit of hopelessness when they find Jesus, are just amazing!

Rachel had spent several years working in India, with close friends Duncan and Vasanti Watkinson, ministering within leper colonies, and amongst orphans, so she had seen desperate poverty and broken people living on the margins of society. But she was beginning to wonder where the next mission's project for Heartcry for Change should be. While Rachel was in Australia, her friend, Margaret Stunt, spoke to her about a lady called Sharon Eason who was working in Molodva and needed pastoral and leadership support. She asked Rachel if she would be willing to connect with Sharon on her return to the UK. Unbeknown to Rachel, at the same time, Helen Azer, Rachel's Associate, was fulfilling a speaking engagement back in the UK on Rachel's behalf. In the coffee break, Helen met a very interesting missionary who was back from the mission field on a short break in England. This lady was called Sharon Eason from Moldova! As Helen talked with her, and heard about the recent women's conference in Moldova at which Margaret Stunt had been a speaker, Helen said to Sharon, "You should meet my colleague, Rachel, who is a great friend of Margaret's. You'd love her and, in fact, I think they're having coffee together in Australia today!" Later, when Rachel rang Helen, they both talked about Moldova and a lady called Sharon Eason! They quickly realized that God was up to something and building divine connections!

On her first visit to Moldova, Rachel saw poverty and conditions in Europe that shocked her deeply and this confirmed that, if anywhere needed a Heartcry for Change, this was it. Gill and Paul Trevor, part of the Heartcry team, helped set up the Heartcry Moldova project, and, over the years, we have had the thrill of watching many broken people being restored. By supporting several missions' couples who are now based in Moldova, we have been able to see embryo church planting and practical outreach: from building homes, drilling wells, supplying vehicles and giving trauma counselling to sharing about Jesus.

Perhaps the project which has moved me the most is the building of the "Princess Academies" which they have set up to rescue young teenage girls who are at risk of being trafficked as sex slaves or who are being abused. At the other end of the scale, is the home to accommodate the older women who have passed their "sell-by date" of usefulness: many are just dumped back in a Moldovan village, with no support, and some of these are now being looked after in a beautiful care home, Casa Helen. I was so touched reading the final phrase in the Heartcry Moldova report online: "There are moments in history when people are given an opportunity to bring transformation and we have decided we must walk through these doors and write history."

From our time in Watford, we had connected relationally with the Message Trust but had also watched the formation of the New Hope Trust to reach the homeless and the many addicts whom we met on the streets. Britain is now the drugs capital of Europe, with higher levels of cocaine and amphetamine abuse than anywhere else in the EU. We have the highest number of drugs-related deaths in Europe, which accounted for 31% of all drug related deaths among 28 EU nations, twice that of the next highest rate of 15% in Germany. Isn't it like God to choose the place of greatest darkness, to let His light shine! It was thrilling to be part of the growth of this ministry, which grew to such a place of influence in the community, that the council, police and social services all commended New Hope Trust for demonstrating the caring heart of Watford.

Once I had taken up my role as the Associate Minister in St Aldate's, Oxford, I found myself being drawn again to the marginalized, and one of the ministries I had to oversee was called ACT (Aldates Community Transformation). It was exciting to see the homeless welcomed into church, but it had its challenging moments too! One of the homeless men had to come in with his dog, and another had a habit of coming up to the front and demanding to talk on the microphone – it was rough, colourful and never dull! One of the highlights was seeing the salvation of one of the main drug dealers in the town and it was our Church Verger who led him to the Lord. He came in one day in tears and just said he couldn't go on living: his life was constantly in such danger and he was at the end of the road. The transformation in this man was astonishing as he allowed Jesus into his life, and he radiated with joy and new hope.

I will never forget the day we trusted our converted drug dealer with the mic during one of our lunchtime gatherings with the homeless. "Hey, listen guys! You all know me, and there's nothing I can hide from you about my past; but guys, this is the real deal! I have been with these people for these last few weeks and seriously – there is nothing flaky about this – this is the real deal: Jesus is real, and He has totally changed my life!"

It was through our relationship with Stuart and Irene Bell and the Groundlevel team that we connected with a similar ministry called "Betel" (Bethel in Spanish) which was started by Elliot Tepper. Over the years, Betel has turned so many lives around, helping to restore thousands of broken, homeless, addicted and unemployed men and women. Their residential homes across the UK are now in 12 urban areas and they look after about 400 recovering men and women with their families; they took in almost 900 individuals last year, and 12,000 in the last 22 years.

Rachel and I have formed a close relationship with the Betel directors, Kent and Mary Alice Martin, and we have begun to minister regularly up in Birmingham where they gather all their residents for a full weekend of ministry every two months. For both of us, it is like being back in Africa with Reinhard. This is revival: men and women running to the front, weeping their way through to Jesus! Just being in the Betel atmosphere totally restores one's faith in the power of the blood of Jesus. With so many addiction rehabilitation programmes failing to reach their target of a radically clean lifestyle for eighteen months or longer, Betel, on the other hand, have been able to more than achieve their goals by putting the "Jesus Factor" clearly at the core of their community.

A friend of ours, who is now part of their leadership team, was addicted to heroin for eleven years; he said that he'd been in and out of short-term rehabs, prison, counselling, and methadone programmes, but the problem was that he never learned to live clean. In all their residences, Betel develop healthy relationships which grows a sense of belonging, self-confidence, significance and purpose; and with time to heal on their side, virtually everyone is restored to their children and families, and they finally learn "to live clean". Most also come to personal faith in Jesus in the early stages, and this clearly empowers them to push through every desire to give up and run.

Betel's outlook on recovery is so different. The method is simple and it's powerful – to model freedom. New entrants are not called "patients" or "clients", they're called "residents". They are not coming into a "treatment programme" but a home where they are welcomed into an extended family, run largely by recovered peers. There is no self-focused group therapy, but regular daily "therapeutic" work, building their personal discipline of a work ethic in teams of recovering men or women.

Everyone gets involved with fully commercial businesses such as landscape gardening, the restaurant trade, food catering, office administration, delivery driving, warehousing, salesmanship, furniture restoration, on-line retailing and tree surgery. One such business is called Rising Café, located inside Coventry Cathedral, which was the top recommendation on TripAdvisor! They have now opened another Rising Café in Lincoln, which is again top on TripAdvisor. Last January they had the honour of a Royal visit as Prince William and Kate heard about the restaurant's reputation and asked to hear the stories of transformed lives. They have also been featured in the Parliamentary Review as an example of something that really works!

We cannot underestimate the power that God has placed in the family unit as most of the residents come from broken, toxic homes. So, by joining a home rooted in healthy relationship-building, socially responsible behaviour, and a strong work ethic, they are able to observe and embrace a lifestyle of abstinence, modeled by their peers. I'm in tears every time we are with them, as the grace of God is so unbelievably present all around, and I get blown away by some of their stories.

Amazingly, all this ministry is free of charge, as together their hard work generates about 80% of the funds which Betel needs annually: last year they earned nearly £4.5 million! The approximately 20% remaining was generously donated by friends of the ministry. It is so boldly counter-cultural! The residences are free to enter, and their core value is that no one should be denied help, regardless of their financial means. What is most amazing is that they receive no government funding or benefits and charge no one! It is simply the hard, faithful work of the recovering residents themselves and each new resident is inspired by the examples of the multitude of changed lives all around them. Together, they share the responsibility to transform their own lives and those of others. In this way, the communities are peer led, with the more experienced members mentoring the new residents by example. As the months pass, the rebuilding of trust and confidence inspires hopeless people to take back responsibility for their own lives, and they proudly help pay for their own recovery – the results are life-changing!

So, over this time, God has given us such a passion to watch Him work in the margins of society. We both come back changed every time we are with these precious people. We know we are called to the margins of society, to reach the broken, and we love it.

26

Unblocking The Well Of Miracles And Revival

A group of about thirty leaders were together in Holland, mostly leaders of Arabic churches around Europe, and some from Egypt. We were there praying for three days in response to the massive wave of 1.2 million Syrian refugees flooding into Germany, asking God to show us how to use this opportunity. Our hearts yearned, "Come on, God! Show us the key to seeing a harvest amongst the Syrians."

On the second day, Fadi Krikor, a Syrian German, arrived and began to share with us that God had told him to buy a large monastery down near Munich where he lived and worked as an architect. He had discovered that the oldest Dominican monastery was being sold and so he approached the nuns, asking to purchase it. Initially he was given no hope, as he wasn't a Catholic, but after a few months they called him, "God has spoken to all our nuns worldwide that you should have this monastery. What are you going to use it for?" Fadi was very honest, "Honestly, we have no idea what God wants to do, He just told us to buy a monastery!" Amazingly, the nuns still sold it to him, and he began to seek God about what His plans were for this place of prayer.

It wasn't long before everyone in the meeting recognized the planning department of God once again. God had his hand all over the details and timing of this project, so the monastery was opened, and is called "Father's House for all Nations", working closely with all the Arabic churches around Europe, and supported by one of the largest churches in Cairo and the Egyptian prayer movement. They have been regularly training people in outreach amongst the Syrians and other migrants in Germany and surrounding nations. To date they believe that about seven thousand migrants have been touched by the Gospel!

It has also become a catalyst of prayer and unity amongst the German church leaders, as well as being a springboard for ministry back into Syria and Armenia, honouring Fadi's family roots. It was stories like the purchase of this monastery, so divinely orchestrated, that made the thirty of us in that room feel, "God's got this!", as we prayed together in Germany that day. The God of miracles, signs and wonders was alive and well and ready to work with us and motivate us into action in Europe: God had got a plan!

On a more recent visit to this monastery, a Korean American walked up to me, a man whom I had never met, and gave me a life changing prophetic word. It is unusual to share the details of a personal prophetic word in a book in this way but this word has redirected and positioned me for the next season of God's harnessing on my life. I had already sensed a new harness being placed on me but this word triggered a fresh expectation of the new chapter of God's adventure that was about to open. This was the word:

"This is a season where God is expanding your mind, and everything you knew about God is going to be expanded in a way you've never seen before. You will experience the supernatural in the natural so often that the supernatural will become natural. You are in stage three of what God has called you to do: I saw your life as a rocket ship, and the first booster rocket has fallen off already about twenty years ago, and now you have the second stage booster rocket falling off now: so you are about to get a boost and, though it may feel like you're losing a part of yourself, you're going to drop weights and burdens of ministry and expectation; now you are about to fire again and you are going to get a boost so that you can go into the stratosphere, where you can actually go into orbit.

So, for the first time in your life, you are going to hit that point of convergence where your ten passions and your ten skill-sets meet over here. Even the transition that you are going through now, which might look very different from what you expected, this is what you were created to do: this is going to be THE work that the Lord has created you for. So this is a season to be excited, and God is going to give you the strength of a young man again, and He's going to surround you with young men, and you're going to have twice as much energy as any of them, and you'll run them into the ground.

You don't need to worry about your age or your state right now because the Lord will supply all your needs according to His riches in glory. Your mind has never aged, and you will still have the sharpness of a young boy. So you will not have to be worried about a loss of any fiscal or mental faculties that you need. You'll be able to learn a lot and there will be a grace for that in this season.

Get your traveling shoes on! I just see lots of travelling to the nations in this season. Keep a low profile in the immediate term because the lower your profile, the more people will fall into you in terms of learning about the things of the Spirit, taking you to places that are higher: the lower you go, the higher and farther He will take you. You are not going to be bored, because He won't allow you to retire, He'll only allow you to refire.

He wants to remind you that it's intimacy with the Lord that is the only thing that He truly cares about, not all the ministry: it's only the character and intimacy with the Lord which you have developed here on earth which you'll be able to take with you. You're a great runner, and you can run long distances, but this a season when He wants you to fly: and the only way you can fly is by understanding which way the winds of the Spirit are blowing. "

I was blown away by the accuracy of the word, even with the details of timing, as we had just received a card from the Watford Wellspring Church, the church we had released to Tim and Helen Roberts, celebrating their twenty-year anniversary of leadership, just a few days earlier! But at this moment, I was wrestling with a sense that I needed to transition once again, after seven years, and let go of the Mahabba Network which I had birthed. This word was such a strong confirmation that now was the time to let go. So I processed this transfer of Mahabba, which has now been transitioned to the team, releasing me for the next phase.

With my time uncluttered once again, I did put my travelling shoes back on and took the opportunity to travel with Rachel for three months. Rachel was booked to speak in Malaysia, Singapore, and then around Australia, and finally in several locations in the States. God caught our attention as we landed in Kuala Lumpur, underlining the fact that our times are in his hands. For, it was a divine coincidence, that it just happened to be exactly thirty years to the very day, when the anointing fell on Rachel and she preached her first sermon in that nation! We both had such a deep sense of the significance of this re-entry into Malaysia, and that we were stepping into a new season of flying in the Spirit together.

After the trip around South East Asia, and Australia, we arrived in the States and were soon in Spokane visiting our friends, Craig and

Monie Lotze. We had just been with them earlier in the year, up in the Italian Alps, researching the places where the Waldensian Revival was ignited when a British army officer, John Charles Beckwith, began to teach and preach all through the Alps and slowly the revival penetrated and spread down across Italy. I will never forget the sense of God's presence when we squeezed through a crack in the rocks in these Italian mountains, and made our way down into the cave where the revivalists hid from persecution and went to cry out to God. It was, once again, a reminder of the cost of previous generations who had carried the flames of revival.

Spokane was the place of John G. Lake's greatest legacy of the Healing Rooms, with 250,000 documented healings in a ten-year period. In his youth as a businessman, Craig had been influenced by stories of Lake, when his father unknowingly bought a building plot for their business which had originally been John G. Lake's headquarters. Craig's actual office was now in the same space of the room in which Lake would pray. So Craig began to find himself being drawn to the God of the miraculous, crying out for revival and power, finally opening the Victory Faith Fellowship, which today reflects God's miracle healing flow. Regularly he would visit the grave of John G. Lake during his lunch hour and sit by the grave, desperately praying that this river of great healing revival would be reopened in this generation.

As we listened to these stories, inside both of us there was kindled a desire to see a fresh flow of the miraculous through our own ministry: so our friends took us down to Lake's grave, and we knelt there by the grave and poured our hearts out to God, stirring the healing mantle of God on our lives once again.

As a couple, we have been so privileged to have travelled the nations with Reinhard Bonnke and the CfaN team, and then with Bro Yun with the Back to Jerusalem ministry. We have watched cripples get up out of wheelchairs or drop their crutches and begin to walk, or even run! We have prayed in the deliverance tent and watched countless people being delivered from witchcraft and tormenting spirits. We have witnessed totally blind eyes opening and heard the shrieking cry of, "I can see! I can see!". We have listened, astonished, as people who were deaf and dumb from birth were instantly healed and began to make their first faltering sounds. We have seen deaf ears reopened – not just in Africa and Asia, but right here in Europe: in Norway five women came forward holding their hearing aids and testified that they were healed!

We have also been totally amazed at times at the power of God flowing through Rachel's ministry, as she travels as "Mama Rachel" through the nations, seeing the hand of God touching thousands. The same God who had performed wonders in Africa and India was equally willing and able to perform the same miracles in the Western World. It has taken many years of persistence, but the spiritual climate has shifted, and people's expectation to see God's miraculous power on the streets of our nations has grown.

In India, we had met so many people who had been healed amongst the Zion Fellowship of Churches, which was the network that John Babu had planted with the help of Rachel's dad, and we even had the joy of meeting people who had been raised from the dead! One, whom everyone called "Hallelujah Mary", had been pronounced dead. At her Hindu funeral, however, it was a tradition for people to pray a blessing over the body as the procession passed by. There was one simple young believer who decided to pray for her and, in his spirit, he saw that God wanted him to speak life into her body. So he reached out his hand towards her and commanded life into her body. She sat up immediately – alive. When asked later about this experience, she said that she saw a bright light, and Jesus standing there with a man who was shouting loudly and telling her to come back to life!

Several years later, Rachel was back in Mysore, India, holding some prayer seminars in the city, when she was asked if she would be willing to pray for a family member of one of the pastors. She was willing but the speaking schedule was so busy that no one had managed to find the time to take her to the hospital. Finally, the family contacted the committee and told them that the hospital had said that this man would probably die within a few hours: they pleaded with the pastors to bring Rachel to come and pray a prayer of blessing for him before he died. Rachel just made it to the hospital in time: the man was floating in and out of consciousness and unable to communicate but his wife was with him praying.

As Rachel laid her hands on his feet to pray with him, she immediately heard God speak to her. So Rachel spoke to the wife and said, "God's just shown me something of the past. He showed me that your husband was betrayed by a businessman fifteen years ago and he became bitter. He is dying today because of that wound which has given him heart disease." The wife wept and said it was all true: he had been a pastor, but he had been persuaded by a businessman to invest his money in a scheme which went wrong and he lost everything and had to go back to work as a teacher. He became very bitter and refused to forgive him and slowly he began to lose his health. Now, fifteen years later, he was dying of heart disease.

Although this man was unable to speak, he could still understand what we were saying and respond with a slight squeeze of the hand. So Rachel asked him to squeeze his wife's hand as she prayed through a prayer of forgiveness. Tears began to softly roll down his cheeks as he squeezed her hand at the end of each phrase of the prayer. Then he began to nod too as we continued praying; now his wife was sobbing too. Rachel went back to her accommodation that night but, the next morning, the wife and her family called the pastor: Alan was sitting up in bed and eating and, within two days, he was released from hospital, totally healed!

I don't know about you but we have decided that we must keep stirring these waters, and expect to see these wells of miracles and revival reopened! We are expectant to see a healing revival flowing from the church into our streets and, having heard God's prophetic word to us, we are determined to dig deep and see this well flow again!

27

FINISHING THE RACE – WELL ADJUSTED

As a horse rider, I understand the need for the constant adjustment of the bridle and bit so that the horse responds correctly to your directions. My grandfather was a prize-winning showjumper for Britain, so riding and an understanding of horses was part of our family life. As I consider my life, I realize that God has been gracious enough to gently adjust the bit in my mouth, and let me run, before he has held the reins more tightly and harnessed me in.

Every season of life has demanded a different adjustment in my life's choices and mind-sets. Starting with the various calls to the nations, I learnt to pioneer and facilitate, worship and intercede, to preach, heal and deliver, to comfort, provide hope and shepherd – so many different calls and anointings, but they were all trained by the Holy Spirit. But now, what burns in me in this new season, is the task to mentor and father and train the sons and daughters, the next generation, for greatness. I want to come alongside outstanding people and enable them to flourish and fulfil their dreams. With every new call, there are new adjustments and skills that have to be mastered.

I can see the patterns of this training and adjustment throughout the last seasons of my life. Probably the most significant shift was in 1989 when the anointing of God fell on my "little Rachel" in Malaysia. Suddenly I was witnessing a unique anointing on Rachel, which demanded an immediate mindset shift in me. My background of all-male education, followed by all-male military service until I was almost thirty, certainly reinforced a strong chauvinistic perspective within me. Unchallenged, this would have been very destructive for both Rachel and me, if God had not opened my eyes to see His ways. To be honest, there was such a remarkable transformation in Rachel in just one moment when the anointing fell on her in Malaysia, that it wasn't hard for me to recognize the difference between the Rachel I knew as my wife, and mother to my children at home, and the Rachel who stood and ministered and preached. I watched her leading massive crowds in prayer and then preaching to thousands and knew she was born to communicate and preach in this way. What was harder to deal with was the deep-seated chauvinism in the church which refused to yield or change.

I shared honestly in chapter sixteen about the denominational chauvinism we encountered when we took over the leadership of the WHCC churches. Even though we could see some of the problems it caused, it took us time to shift the mindsets and adjust our practice of leadership. Again and again we noticed a repetitive occurrence after our elders' meetings! After our all-male meetings, we would go home and chat to our wives about the decisions we had made, and then the wives would point out some legitimate, practical issues we had overlooked. This meant that we would return the following week and, one by one, we would each comment, "I'm afraid what we planned isn't going to work, as we hadn't thought of this problem." It was amusing and, before long, we knew we needed the wisdom of our wives helping us to make good choices! This unbending chauvinistic mindset had to go and we needed to be free to run together. We were so blessed that Tony Morton and CNet provided a wider framework for our church in those days, as we left the other network.

It has been a wonderful learning curve as Rachel and I have learnt to flow and alternate together as either a Priscilla-Aquila or Aquila-Priscilla couple in the nations. It does not come overnight, and both of us have had to learn how to sense the lead of the Holy Spirit and recognize who is best gifted to lead in that particular moment. What has been essential for us both, is discovering how our main gifts work and dove-tail together, and then trusting and leaning into our understanding of who we are.

My gift is very much as a facilitator, builder and pastor, while Rachel's gifting has been more the pioneering and prophetic. In practice, this means that Rachel will often have a clear understanding of what God wants to do about two years before it happens, when I can see nothing; but when it gets close to the timing of this event, she has often forgotten what she felt, but I have to lead and direct the hands-on application and facilitation of what she sensed. Prophets have to process the word they carry too! So, although Rachel can prophesy and sense the shift and season of change, she admits openly that she herself personally hates living through the resulting process of change! This complexity of working with each other's gifts can result in the unveiling of many personal insecurities and wounds. If the wife is the pioneer, she can feel she is taking the initiative and so dominating her husband and feel guilty. Or, as a husband, you can feel that you are being bossed and not taking the appropriate lead and so overreact. This is where trust and communication are so vital. As a couple, harnessed together for ministry, we need to lead from the place of peace, both knowing and honouring what God is calling us to do, but also understanding which part of the call we are each called to lead and when.

It has been a joy to watch the partnership of Rachel and Helen Azer develop. Again they have different skills and, although both are strong prophetic preachers, Rachel will defer to Helen whenever the situation requires a detailed, teaching input. It has also been interesting for Helen and I to work together too, and discover how our gifts can best be harnessed together in the ministry. It takes a different adjustment for us to flow together, than the way I work with Rachel, though it is just as impacting. For most of my life, it has been an unwritten assumption that women can carry the prophetic ministry, but men should always be the apostolic leaders. However, increasingly, I have watched a few churches receive Rachel as both a prophetic and apostolic voice to their leadership team. They present the situations they are facing and Rachel will present them with a prophetic blueprint of the next season, or give them an outline of strategic wisdom to help them accomplish their vision.

What always astonishes me is that, if Rachel had been invited into a church for her prophetic wisdom and for some reason is unable to go, I seem to be able to step out of my more pastoral gift into her prophetic gift, and watch as the prophetic miraculously flows! After all, we are all just donkeys for Jesus, carrying Him in all his glory and gifting to minister by the Spirit into every type of place, from the broken and hopeless to those hungry for more of God.

I remember when I worked with Bro Yun, the Heavenly Man, he said that seventy percent of all the evangelists and church planters in the China Revival were women, many of whom were just in their late teens and early twenties! But he also shared that most of the top-level apostolic leaders, who were the overseers of the main movements and networks, were men, but there were some excellent apostolic women who worked with them too. I am excited, looking from our vantage point in Oxford, surrounded by outstanding future world leaders, that we can create a new church culture which releases thousands of women to work alongside men, in a full spectrum of ministries, which God has for them.

As I have been learning to be a father to this next generation, a major adjustment for me has been learning to step back from my more prominent and defined leadership roles and be a support to others as they learn to lead. The harness has shifted and I find myself enjoying the anonymity of being part of the welcome team on the door of our church, unknown in terms of all my past achievements, but loved as the grey-haired man with a smiley face, who loves people. It has been a huge shift from being the Anglican Parish Vicar just five hundred yards down the road in St Aldate's Church with 1000 years of history, to now being on the connections team at the new Hillsong Church in Oxford. Here I am surrounded by the buzz of a new generation, excited as we help harness their lives with a fresh passion for Jesus. I am in a privileged place of gaining their trust as they ask me for advice to run their race and fulfil their dreams.

It has also been one of our greatest joys to see our daughter, Nicola, and our son, David, stepping into the legacy of their spiritual inheritance too. But it does require another adjustment, as I suddenly become aware that our kids are now flowing with their own ministry and authority. They have grown up and are flourishing in their own right! We are both overwhelmed with gratitude as we watch them and our grandkids now leaving their stamp on the world too. In Australia, Nicola and her husband, Tim, have pioneered together in birthing the Melbourne Hillsong churches which have already grown to over 5000 people. Our son, David, is currently Chief Financial Officer of a building and agricultural machinery company in the UK, still holding a call in his heart to express the generosity and kindness of God to the nations through Kingdom finances.

As we see the blessing on our children, I have realized I need to reposition myself and model this biblical moment of transfer which requires the father to bless his children and give them a legacy. Biblically, this moment of transfer happened when the son was aged thirty, known by the Greek word "huios" meaning a mature son, and this moment of transfer was done in a very precise way. Typically, the father would give a party and gather everyone together and declare to them all, "This is my beloved son and heir!" At that moment, all the wealth, inheritance and authority would be legally passed over to this designated son. That is exactly what God the Father did when Jesus reached thirty years of age and came to be baptized and, from that moment, he was able to say that, "all power in heaven and on earth has been given to me". What a privilege to train our natural and spiritual sons and daughters with this understanding!

On my last birthday (aged 67) a thought crossed my mind, "Welcome to the next 53 years of ministry!" I just began to laugh at this impossible thought, as my mind did the maths! However ridiculous it is in terms of life-expectancy, I believe that this is much more about a mental harnessing for adventure, which needs a deep-seated perception that we are just getting started! The greatest years are ahead of us and the best is still to come, and neither Rachel nor I want to miss them!

Last night at our Heart and Soul meeting of our Hillsong Church in Oxford, I saw in my spirit a huge wave that was carrying us out into the deep ocean. I knew that, like Holy Spirit surfers, we need to have our eyes fixed on the horizon so that we harness these waves and carry this power to the nations. I felt God speaking to me from the passage in Ezekiel chapter forty-seven. It's not enough to be in this water ankle-deep, knee-deep, or even waist-deep at this time. To catch this wave, you need to be totally committed to the wave, totally out of your depth, one hundred percent given and ready to ride this extreme wave of God!

Let's get ready and make sure that we are fully harnessed with an incredible God, and get prepared for the greatest of all adventures!

BOOKS BY RACHEL HICKSON

I ♡ PRAYER
Connected to God, Changing the World

Release My
Frozen Assets
A look at the role of women in the church

EAT THE WORD
SPEAK THE WORD

STEPPING STONES TO

FREEDOM

A 40 DAY DEVOTIONAL

Pathway of
A 40 DAY DEVOTIONAL   Peace

Run Your Race
SOMETHING TO LIVE FOR!

All books available through

www.heartcryforchange.com/shop

225

Printed in Great Britain
by Amazon

20271521R00129